"THEN THE DISCIPLES CAME AND SAID TO HIM, 'WHY DO YOU SPEAK TO THEM IN PARABLES?'"

David A. Redding

THE PARABLES HE TOLD

IT IS IN THE MIDDLE OF THE NIGHT. YOU ARE ASLEEP. THE HOUSE IS AFIRE AND FILLED WITH SMOKE. SUDDENLY JESUS AWAKENS YOU AND SAYS: "COME WITH ME TO SAFETY. I DO NOT HAVE TIME TO EXPLAIN EVERYTHING NOW." HIS PARABLES DO NOT EXPLAIN EVERYTHING, BUT THEY GIVE SUFFICIENT DIRECTIONS TO GET US OUT OF THE DOOMED HOUSE AFTER HIM.

From the book

HARPER JUBILEE BOOKS

THE PARABLES HE TOLD

David A. Redding

HARPER & ROW, PUBLISHERS

NEW YORK, HAGERSTOWN,

SAN FRANCISCO, LONDON

To my
father and mother
and my little sister

FIRST HARPER & ROW PAPERBACK EDITION PUBLISHED IN 1976.

ISBN: 0-06-066813-x

LIBRARY OF CONGRESS CATALOG CARD NUMBER: 76-9972

Preface

God gave Jesus some Good News. What could He put it in to keep it safe and fresh? What would be the most practical cup to serve it in at any time or place? Homer had an Iliad, Paul used letters, Aesop fables, and Shakespeare plays, to put their thinking in. Christ's choice was in perfect taste. He picked up and polished to perfection an old container the prophets had left behind: the parable. He hid His treasure in this—safely for all time, simply for all ages. He stirred God's Word in it in such a way as to make it a surprise appropriate for shepherds and kings, something to love and cherish always. Today, after almost two thousand years, what He said is still sparkling, tempting, sacred. Shakespeare, in a short time, has become almost the exclusive property of the educated. But the parables of the Mustard Seed, of the Good Samaritan, of a Sower Going Out To Sow, still belong to all of us.

What is a parable? A fable is a fantastic tale with trees and foxes speaking. A proverb is a statement with no tale at all. An allegory is a story with each part robotlike, standing for something. But a parable is a story true to this house of earth, but with a window open to the sky. One can get lost in the details, but the aim is to find the "big idea" and as Chrysostom said, "Be not overbusy about the rest." Jesus' recipe: A favorite story on a familiar subject and a flash of heavenly light.

"Then the disciples came and said to him, 'Why do you speak to them in parables?' And he answered them, 'To you it has been given to know the secrets of the kingdom of heaven, but to them it has not been given. For to him who has will more be given, and he will have in abundance; but from him who has not, even what he has will be taken away. This is why I speak to them in parables, because seeing they do not see, and hearing they do not hear, nor do they understand' " (Matthew 13:10-13). As Matthew Henry has said, "The parables are the cloud wherein the Great Teacher descended." The meaning of the passage is difficult to penetrate. Of course the gospel truth is something hidden from the wise and revealed to babes. It will not make sense to the stubborn but goes straight to the heart of the sons of light. He is not trying to lock up His secret but to break the lock on the hardened hearts of men with words that would shock them into seeing how blind they were. He quotes Isaiah saying the same thing for the same reason in Matthew 13:14-16. These words were not said to damn men but to get results.

Perhaps it can be said that the parable is the shell He gives His seed to protect it from overexposure and disinterest. He would keep His secret in parabolic code to hide it from those who merely wished to play with it, and so no one would be forced-fed or know more than he wanted to know. Furthermore, plain speech would have provoked more ridicule from His enemies and less thought from His friends. Pouring His gospel into parables roused His followers to search for more meaning and made it possible for Him to take His opponent by surprise. He could win the sympathy of His adversary with a story that would stir the man to believe and be better before he realized he had been struck.

But Jesus used parables not so much to protect His secret as to project it. They illustrated His gospel, made it popular, not academic. These parables belong not to the theologian but to the poet, and most of all to the people, "the people who walk in darkness." "All this Jesus said to the crowds in parables; indeed he said nothing to them without a parable. This was to fulfil what was spoken by the prophet: 'I will open my mouth in parables, I will utter what has been hidden, since the foundation of the world' " (Matthew 13:34,35). Jesus wanted to tell us ". . . everything I have been told by my Father." But He was brief and able to speak volumes in a few verses. And the Son did not blast the earth with one explosion of light. He let it dawn on men in these parables. He made them like stained glass so men would not be

vi

blinded but blessed with color. They would capture the attention as a picture but hold it as a painting, give everything away, but not give it all away at once or to one age. His stories would release His light slowly like stars—enough to last a lifetime and for all time.

A distinguished rabbi friend of mine, a professor in one of the finest divinity schools in the world, used to tease me for presenting Jesus as The Master Teller of Parables. He insisted that Jesus was simply a Teller of Parables; so I asked him to come up with competitive samples from rabbinic teaching. While everyone is aware that this is a common middle eastern literary form, it amused me that no parables worth repeating came to his mind at that moment.

At our next meeting he had unearthed one from the Midrash, the storehouse of rabbinic commentary on the Scriptures. This particular example was told by the rabbis to illustrate Proverbs 21:18, which reads: "Death and Life are in the power of the tongue."

There was a king who had an illness that no one could cure. He consulted his physicians and court officials in vain. Finally, a seer appeared who claimed that the illness of the king could be cured by the milk of a lioness.

A man came forward who accepted the awesome assignment of finding and milking a lioness. He succeeded, and upon returning from the quest, he fell asleep under a tree, during which time the members of his body had an argument over which one had been more important. The fingers felt they were since they had done the milking. The feet insisted they had taken the necessary steps, and so on...The tongue announced, to the consternation of the other members of the body, that it had the power of life and death. All the other members jeered.

When the man came before the king, he found himself saying to his horror: "O King, I have brought you the milk of a goat." He was peremptorily thrown into the dungeon to await execution, where, during his next nap, the other members of the body quickly paid tribute to the tongue's power of life and death, so that the poor prisoner was able to correct his report to the king and save his life.

The story makes its point, but it is no parable. It is a fable. Hands and feet have no speaking parts; and furthermore, Jesus would never tell so farfetched a tale. His artistry was never bizarre, but always breathtakingly close to home. As a great artist does, Jesus shaped his masterpieces from scenes we can immediately recognize as strangely familiar.

There is only one parable I know of that rivals the quality of the parables He told, and I must tell it here in context because it illustrates so beautifully the purpose of the parables and the way Jesus practiced them. I believe this to be the particular parable that instructed Christ in the art and decided Him to choose parables as His method of preaching, for it broke the heart rightly of a man who was both a shepherd and a king.

One spring instead of going to war, David remained in Jerusalem. He noticed a beautiful woman bathing, and sent for her. She was named Bathsheba. In order to conceal his deed he had her husband, Uriah, brought back from the battlefront. But Uriah was vowed for battle for the Lord of Hosts and refused to sleep with his wife during his royal furlough, even though the king made him drunk. Finally, in desperation, King David returned him to the battlefront with word to Joab, his general, to place Uriah in the forefront of the fighting—then to order the rest of the army to fall back so Uriah would be killed.

The deed was done. This was all in a day's work for kings in those days. But as the Book of Samuel notes, "There was a God in Israel."

So a country preacher named Nathan gained an audience with the king. Perhaps, as Kierkegaard suggests, David felt Nathan wanted to learn some pointers from the great Psalmist king. How kind of the spiritual ruler of all Israel to coach this rural novice in his profession. But Nathan wanted to report to the king about a rich man who had many flocks and herds who happened to live next door to a poor man who had nothing but one ewe lamb, which lived in his tent, ate from his morsel, and drank from his bowl. The rich man had guests and in order to feed them he killed the poor man's one ewe lamb.

At this point in Nathan's brief narrative, King David cried, "That rich man deserves to die," whereupon Nathan said, "O King, thou art the man."

Had Nathan condemned the king outright for his behavior, he might have had his throat slit—certainly he would not have disarmed the king. But by putting it in story form, King David condemned the villain before he realized it was himself. Then David went out and repented in sackcloth and ashes. Here is much of the artistry of the parable. Jesus did not go about reproaching people. He pictured the problem in stories, then permitted people to pin it on themselves if they were ready. Those who were not ready were not pushed.

As with Nathan, Jesus used parables at times when any other method would have brought death. But by these stories, he escaped the wrath of hostile audiences and pricked the hearts of those whose time had come to change. Never was psychology put to better use. Through parables a listener is able to this day to be changed, not by force, but from the inside out.

The villain in the New Testament is not Judas, according to the parables of Jesus. Time after time the villain turns out to be the kind of person depicted by the elder brother—as Mark Twain called him, "The good man in the worst sense of the word." In the story of the good Samaritan, the villain is the priest himself. Jesus' most common villain typically performs the treason described by T. S. Eliot as "doing the right thing for the wrong reason." Instead of being in God's pocket, he has God in his pocket. He is letter perfect, but he is heartless. He is using religion to save his own skin and to show off.

The parable of the pharisee and publican praying highlights Jesus' hatred of this pride and how inescapable pride is. The pharisee publicly thanks God for being better than other men, in particular for not being like that tax collector standing nearby. But Christ scorned such arrogance and approved the tax collector who would not so much as lift his eyes to heaven, but prayed: "Lord, be merciful to me a sinner." According to Augustine there are only three requirements to be a Christian: (1) humility, (2) humility, and (3) humility. That is the point of view of the parables. And how impossible it is for us. As one Sunday school teacher said immediately after she had told the children about the pharisee and the publican: "Now children, let us thank God we are not like that pharisee." I am thankful that I am not like that teacher, and on it goes.

The Bible is a mirror, as Søren Kierkegaard says, but we prefer to weigh or measure the mirror rather than see ourselves as we really are. We often use scholarship to distract us or to dull the terrifying reality of our reflection. It is so much easier to count the cracks and to look up the age of this mirror, than to look into it. Kierkegaard offers guidance in how to read the parables. For instance, when we are reading the story of the good Samaritan we shouldn't say: "A priest went by on the other side"—instead say: "I went by." Then when the good Samaritan comes by, just so you won't get bored always saying "I," say: "This is not I."

Just as Nathan's parable of the poor man's one ewe lamb was told on his audience, so it is for the reader of Christ's parables to this day: "You are the man!"—although Christ permits the reader to say: "I am the man."

Throughout the parables runs the note of urgency. If I were to offer a parable of my own to illustrate our life situation according to the parables, it would go something like this:

It is in the middle of the night. You are asleep. The house is afire and filled with smoke. Suddenly Jesus awakens you and says: "Come with me to safety. I do not have time to explain everything now." His parables do not explain everything, but they give sufficient directions to get us out of the doomed house after Him.

The parables are perfect for today. They are the particular legacy He left for the twentieth century when it ran low of faith —as if He knew exactly what we needed, even to our taste in religion. For these stories are completely free of the religious vocabulary that seems so offensive to our critical age. He speaks here, as everywhere, "as one having authority," but wears His mantle so modestly, so becomingly, and speaks our language so well and in such a way that no one could be antagonized. Easterner though He was, He left enough room in these stories for anyone's interpretation, but enough salvation to disarm the whole sophisticated world from East to West. His parables are so apt for us right now, and so much of their meaning has been lying around, never unwrapped, it is as if He had marked them, "Not to be opened until the space age."

In this book I have tried to make the parables come to life, to show what thumping good stories they are and what incomparable masterpieces of literature. And above all I have tried not to interfere with their authority, for they are gospel not meant merely to be dissected and loved, but obeyed.

Each parable is presented at the beginning of the chapter that bears its name, just as it appears in Holy Writ. I have used a number of different versions of the Bible to do this, depending upon which version seemed to serve that parable best. No one can deny that the words from the King James have a special sacramental force for those of us familiar with its lordly language since childhood, so I have used it in many of the more familiar parables and find that I keep falling back into it in chapters introduced by another version. But the plain truth is that some of the parables simply are not clear in Elizabethan English, or do not quite say to today's reader what they said to King James. In those cases I have found the New English Bible and some of the other versions a much better choice. Perhaps the use of different versions of the Bible will help express the infinite variety of the parables and show less disrespect to their hoary age and do less damage to their youthful freshness than the rigid use of one version.

Jesus told forty parables, and I felt that each should be permitted to appear in a book of this kind. There are a number of "parable germs," as Bruce called them, which are not included in this work.

His parables come to us just as they left His lips, for they were too well made to lose their original shape; in them we can see with His eyes the tiny scenes He saw here below which illumine the world that He saw best above.

> What if earth
> Be but the shadow of heaven, and things therein,
> Each to the other like, more than on earth is thought?
> —*John Milton*

David A. Redding
Glendale, Ohio

Acknowledgment

While I am indebted, directly or indirectly, to anyone who has ever written anything on the subject of the parables, I am especially grateful for the Exegesis in *The Interpreter's Bible* and for the inspiration and insight provided by such standard works as A. B. Bruce's *The Parabolic Teaching of Christ,* R. C. Trench's *Notes on the Parables of Our Lord,* and to Dr. George Buttrick's little classic, *The Parables of Jesus,* to which anyone who wants a scholarly introduction to the parables must turn. Among the other works listed in the bibliography I would recommend particularly those by A. T. Cadoux and C. H. Dodd.

I am deeply indebted to Mrs. Houghton R. Rouff for many laborious hours of overtime spent in typing the manuscript. The Reverend Paul McKenna, Mrs. Martin P. Cary, and the Reverend Merwyn W. Glandon read the manuscript and made many valuable suggestions for which I am very grateful. My father-in-law, John Maxwell McCleery, M.D., added immeasurably to my standing debt of a wife by correcting the completed manuscript and offering reassuring encouragement. With affection and pride I mention my wife whose tireless proofreading, imaginative ideas, and never-failing encouragement made it possible for me to write a book. At last I come to you, my reader, hoping you will have patience with me and permit me now to ask heaven that this edition of *The Parables He Told* may bring you to the Author Himself who remains after all these years, not merely our Poet Laureate, but "the Author and Finisher of our faith."

Contents

CONTENTS

I

This Is Your God

THEN drew near unto him all the publicans and sinners for to hear him. And the Pharisees and scribes murmured, saying, This man receiveth sinners, and eateth with them. And he spake this parable unto them, saying, What man of you, having an hundred sheep, if he lose one of them, doth not leave the ninety and nine in the wilderness, and go after that which is lost, until he find it? And when he hath found it, he layeth it on his shoulders, rejoicing. And when he cometh home, he calleth together his friends and neighbours, saying unto them, Rejoice with me; for I have found my sheep which was lost. I say unto you, that likewise joy shall be in heaven over one sinner that repenteth, more than over ninety and nine just persons, which need no repentance. Either what woman having ten pieces of silver, if she lose one piece, doth not light a candle, and sweep the house, and seek diligently till she find it? And when she hath found it, she calleth her friends and her neighbours together, saying, Rejoice with me; for I have found the piece which I had lost. Likewise, I say unto you, there is joy in the presence of the angels of God over one sinner that repenteth.

LUKE 15:1-10, King James Version

✞

AND he said, A certain man had two sons: And the younger of them said to his father, Father, give me the portion of goods that falleth to me. And he divided unto them his living. And not many days after the younger son gathered all together, and took his journey into a far country, and there wasted his substance with riotous living. And when he had spent all, there arose a mighty famine in that land; and he began to be in want. And he went and joined himself to a citizen of that country; and he sent him into his fields to feed swine. And he would fain have filled *his belly with the husks that the swine did eat: and no man gave unto him. And when he came to himself, he said, How many hired servants of my father's have bread enough and to spare, and I perish with hunger! I will arise and go to my father, and will say unto him, Father, I have sinned against heaven, and before thee, And am no more worthy to be called thy son: make me as one of thy hired servants. And he arose, and came to his father. But when he was yet a great way off, his father saw him, and had compassion, and ran, and fell on his neck, and kissed him. And the son said unto him, Father, I have sinned against heaven, and in thy sight, and am no more worthy to be called thy son. But the father said to his servants, Bring forth the best robe, and put it on him; and put a ring on his hand, and shoes on his feet: And bring hither the fatted calf, and kill it; and let us eat, and be merry: For this my son was dead, and is alive again; he was lost, and is found. And they began to be merry. Now his elder son was in the field: and as he came and drew nigh to the house, he heard musick and dancing. And he called one of the servants, and asked what these things meant. And he said unto him, Thy brother is come; and thy father hath killed the fatted calf, because he hath received him safe and sound. And he was angry, and would not go in: therefore came his father out, and intreated him. And he answering said to his father, Lo, these many years do I serve thee, neither transgressed I at any time thy commandment: and yet thou never gavest me a kid, that I might make merry with my friends: But as soon as this thy son was come, which hath devoured thy living with harlots, thou hast killed for him the fatted calf. And he said unto him, Son, thou art ever with me, and all that I have is thine. It was meet that we should make merry, and be glad: for this thy brother was dead, and is alive again; and was lost, and is found.*

LUKE 15:11-32, King James Version

The Lost Sheep
The Lost Coin
The Prodigal Son

LOST: ONE PLANET with some people still on it. *Man overboard* in a sea of space and the man is Everyman. Lost: The Faith of Our Fathers—in a bottomless pit of cold suspicion and very scholarly research. Lost: Late last night, I'm afraid, up the tortuous streets of science, in the relativity of the times, somewhere in the mushrooming mountain of stacks at the library, in the desolate miles of files. Lost: Broken under the nervewracking ultimatums of a Bear and his nuclear six-shooters fired at the feet enough to make a nation dance a jig. Lost: In the killing pace of progress, the runaway race for status. Lost: Carried out by a floodtide of pleasure, chased by the man-eating sharks inside himself, picked to pieces by analysis. Lost: Last seen somewhere east of Eden, a man whose name is Adam. Lost: His God, His Garden, His Way.

What do we do now? Is there anything written on the subject? Luke found three "lost" stories for us in his fifteenth chapter. It is the greatest collection extant. They are not maps but masterpieces. They are not much, but they are everything—not popular, but to a precious few perhaps "a find." We do not look in here for something new, but for any news at all of an old friend. Someone who has lost something does not go on, but goes back over everything again. If you have lost anything important, like yourself, it is time to "Look Homeward Angel." This takes us back to those gentle hints He illustrated in Holy Writ that this book is about and with a prayer begins.

"Now all the publicans and sinners were drawing near unto

him to hear him." Jesus got into bad company very quickly. This was not an isolated incident, but a conspicuous habit. The New Testament is sprinkled heavily with shady characters. He appeared with them in public and took His meals with them. It caused a scandal which helped to wreck His career and bring Him to an early grave.

"Both the Pharisees and the scribes" snarled and tried to corner Him. Instead of bitterness, it drew from Him the most disarming and incontrovertible of all His wonderful ideas.

"What man of you having a hundred sheep." The story gives God away immediately, and what He does for a living. Who is God? That question today trips a variety of clichés. Vast amounts of erudition are wasted in evasion. A man will concede he believes in God, then qualify to death the inch he gave. God is not Someone any more, but an it, a kind of cosmic muscle, a tendency, perhaps a principle, a quilt put together from the pieces of old gods to try and please everybody. In the stereotyped drydock discussion God disappears into thin air and becomes less real, less revered, than a childhood sweetheart. The term is kept, out of respect for the Great Books. It is a good word for the unknown, an indulgence shown to the Vanishing American. But the professor with characteristic detachment smilingly implies: "Every god has his day."

This point of view is adolescent and naïve to the Teacher. He was too well informed to accept that prehistoric hypothesis, and spoke from deep experience. The Lord was not a nobody to Him, nor a retired landscape architect. "The Lord is my shepherd." He is not the obsolete ignition system that started existence. A.D. does not mean after working hours for the Creator. God does not do less as He nears the deadline. Right now becomes the busiest part of His day so far. What makes us think we would be permitted into consciousness completely unsupervised? How do we deserve any more credit for our prosperity than the sparrows do for theirs? Have we not noticed the hand that feeds us, looks after us—Someone with more sense than sheep? Whose fault is it if mankind looks "like sheep without a shepherd"?

We do not have to follow our noses. "He leadeth me in the paths of righteousness." God was not simply a temporary policy to pull men through the Middle Ages—not simply a stone, a symbol for baptisms, weddings, despite the Cave Man's deadening influence. God is on the job, at breakfast, during fall-out, the ball game, and all the way—"Yea, though I walk through the valley of the shadow of death. . . ."

The solid citizens were screaming at Him for slumming and He silenced them forever with this story: "What man of you, having a hundred sheep, and having lost one of them, doth not leave the ninety and nine in the wilderness, and go after that which is lost. . . ?" Everyone leaves everything to look for so little a thing as his hat. Now what would you do if you were God and lost some men that belonged to you? What could be more natural than for God to look for His lost men who look for their lost hats? If "all we like sheep have gone astray" in this world, off course in reef-filled waters, and in the devastating darkness we are fighting frantically for our very lives and sanity, it all means we mean not less to Him but more. He is a good God in an emergency. We wash our hands of runaways, but God is not Pilate and feels responsible for us. He is up in the middle of this very dark night and on His way. He does not freeze nor die from fright like sheep and He is equipped for rescues with more than ram's horns, lamb's brains. Above the blasts of our nuclear tests is a sound too high for human frailty and fear. But faith can hear at times the echoing footfalls, and feel the earth trembling from the approaching steps of the Almighty, coming

> . . . with unhurrying chase
> And unperturbed pace,
> Deliberate speed, majestic instancy,

to the rescue of His helplessly, hopelessly lost and panicked sheep.

The Author never once charges sin in this whole story. His word for that is "lost." We like to call ourselves sinners; something makes us think there's glamour in it. It identifies us at the

7

club as one of the boys. It boasts that I'm not boasting goodness. We are fooling ourselves. Sin is why and what happens when a man loses his sense of direction. And that is hard to own up to. No man likes to confess he's lost. It's unmanly, humiliating, and a man will do anything, but everything, to prove he's not a baby any more. So like some big chief we cover up: "Indian not lost. Wigwam lost." But God knows and we know; so do others just the same. We have sailed too far out and, frankly, can't see land and are at the mercy of a squeaking mast and God.

The commotion our condition causes heaven, and the trouble God goes to to recover us is a special assignment of this story's twin. "Or what woman having ten pieces of silver, if she lose one piece, doth not light a lamp, and sweep the house . . . diligently. . . ?" The verses reflect the intensity of God's interest for the lost. Heaven appears here totally absorbed in the lost and lets everything else go to get them back. This cannot wait until morning. She lights a lamp. She will not stop with a casual investigation. She makes the dust fly. God will not be distracted by the rest of His smoothly running universe until this planet is safely in its place again. The Mastermind is not resting on His laurels, not satisfied with His saints, nor musing sleepily over the things in good working order. The important thing to Him, just this minute, is to find the precious missing parts. His eye is riveted on the vulnerable point where Creation is breaking down and blowing away.

The second story is more practical—more promising. In contrast to one solitary shepherd against the wilderness, this woman has only one house to go through. The story calls to mind a more carefully planned and more extensive campaign—a thorough housecleaning from top to bottom. It is a challenging task, but the coin is in there somewhere and she is sweeping painstakingly, furiously. Will God give up any one of His children for lost with any less effort and determination than a poor woman trying to locate her sixteen-cent piece?

"If she lose one piece. . . ." All three of these stories told by Luke shout "one" at once. Duped as we are by size, doped all our lives by the idea that more and bigger is better, we cannot get a God of quantity out of our heads. It is so hard for us to see how God, with all His constellations of stars and succession of civilizations, could care a fingersnap for "little old me." But only little gods are impressed by Gargantua. Our God picks up things invisible to Thor. This God is very careful about His snowflakes, even patterning His universe after the structure of His atoms. Unlike Ashtarte, He is a family man. Tiny Tim means more to Him than any golden mountain. This is the God who made man after His own heart and sent His only Son into the world a microscopic cell.

But this lost piece of silver betrays His weakness for the low even more than the least—for the black, not merely the lost, sheep. Apparently, even more important to Him than creating is refinishing, reclaiming a man—the second creation. Perhaps His pride is at stake, His ability, His original workmanship called into question, His integrity as a craftsman of men, but most of all a Father's heart. While our age has thought of God mainly as Creator, these stories show Him more interested in repair and maintenance, carrying through creation to completion.

The "lost coin" clears man of a part of the guilt for getting lost. The coin didn't get lost by itself. A hand dropped it. Which is to say another way that no man bears all the blame for his sin. God knows. Certainly Fagin was at fault for little Oliver. What father would say his example is perfectly safe for his son? Mankind is all mixed up in this together. But each man must bear his share, including all the shallow times he has said, "It's not my fault."

This is no encouragement to carelessness—for going down a crack or into the woods. Being lost is no fun—witness the Dorian Grays, the faces in distress. Despite the phony frosting, sin is poisonous. And it is habit forming. If it is an adventure it is the adventure of the castaway—the suffering and the chances of sighting land together make it a pitiful experiment, and a dirty trick to play on any search party.

"And seek diligently until she finds it." This does not mean lost men will be recovered as a matter of course. Redemption is not routine, but rather a death struggle with the devil. The Bible is a warning as well as a promise posted to this planet's visitors: "Travel at your own risk." "We pray 'Thy will be done' because it might not otherwise be done." Unlike heaven, this world is up in the air. "Life is real! Life is earnest!"—not automatic. Our traitorous wills can block the best that God can do. "How often," He said, "would I have gathered your children together as a hen gathers her brood under her wings, and you would not!"

But the phrase "seek diligently until she finds it," is a lifesaver in itself. Someone cares and will not quit as long as there is still more work to do. God's aim is not creation but perfection. He is not satisfied with a good harvest; He wants every planted seed present and accounted for. Ninety-nine are not enough. Love cannot rest until that last one is in from "the hills away far off from the gates of gold." These stories and their signature make us more suspicious than anything else ever written, that there is, after all, a love "that wilt not let me go."

The effect this idea has on us is electric. It brings necessary relief and resources to fight, not resignation to inevitable judgment. It does not take away our responsibility but takes away the oppression of isolation and futility that breaks the spirit. It offers the comfort and encouragement man is starving for in the frightening few minutes we're all having these days. It is something to keep us from wanting to lie down and die, to keep us going, to get us through this; to get through to us that, despite the hard, cold facts, we have not been abandoned to our own devices, that our horizons do not include a full picture of all the help we're getting and is coming soon.

"And when he hath found it, he layeth it on his shoulders. . . ." This is news, a new picture for us of Judgment Day. When the shepherd arrived on the scene, He did not have the time nor heart to say, "I told you so." It seemed time to Him for judgment to stop and step aside for sympathy. He brings, instead of the tears and gnashing teeth, the seat of honor, a special treat, "on his shoulders," to help the shivering wanderer forget the wolves. God is not the Secret Police but a shepherd, our suffering servant, our physician, our friend. Who knows what He's gone through for us? We lamely say, "A cross," and that He "Seekest us through pain." What did Isaiah mean? "Surely He hath borne our griefs, and carried our sorrows, . . . He was wounded for our transgressions, . . . and the Lord hath laid on him the iniquity of us all." It all makes the millennium seem a little less forbidding, into a good time for a show of affection, mothering. It may not be less heartbreaking, because "we were bought with a price."

"Rejoicing." The scene gives us a glimpse of God without the frowning Puritan face—eyes wet not with reproach but happiness. God is just and honest. These stories do not mean to make anyone miscalculate His righteous indignation. "The fear of the Lord is the beginning of wisdom," but wisdom sees in the end that He can dance, He can sing. This Father knows how to enjoy Himself and His children. The weary shepherd and the hardworking woman were thrilled to see their lost sheep and missing silver once again. Imagine God's excitement, if late some night looking through the wilderness He comes across the lad He lost, ages ago it seems. When we see God, we shall see Him as He is, and these two stories insist, we shall see Him smiling.

A find is too good for God to keep, and not even glory can take it in its stride. God knows just what will interest saints and please heaven. He is the life of the party there and knows just when to fling His crown for joy, how to make the angels laugh, for they are all soul-centered. This is the news they are interested in up high. This is the word they have been waiting for, praying for, working for—*Found*. So, "There will be more joy in heaven over one sinner who repents. . . ."

His finest parable is about a father and his boy. It has worn smooth with telling, but the newness has not worn off. It is still provoking, puzzling, and its ending as shocking and un-

11

believably wonderful as it was to those who heard it in the beginning. It is the priceless gem of His gospel, yet everyone in the Bible forgot to tell it to us with one exception. Luke remembered. It is a Christian education. In one short, staggering assignment it almost gives away the secret of the Kingdom, and of all the things that have ever been written it comes closest to giving us a glimpse of the hallowed face of God.

"A certain man had two sons." "A certain man" is the hero, not his son. This story has been called incorrectly. Its proper name: "The Perfect Father." It has been missent to the wrong address. The church has said it to a select audience of black sheep, and Jesus meant it for everybody. "A certain man had two sons." That's all God has—except His perfect One. You and I are either prodigal, Pharisee—or perfect. There is no other breed of man. All mankind falls into one or both of these categories. His plot was expertly designed to catch us all off guard—rich and poor, father and son, the boy who never left home as well as the one who ran away. The cast is a group picture of the whole family of man. If we have missed seeing ourselves, we have missed the point, for it doesn't miss a man.

"And the younger of them said to his father, Father, give me. . . ." Those were his first words, the first words of every fallen son of man, back of every boyhood fight. His son did not say, "What can I give you?" He never thought of his father's wishes nor the will of God. He did not care, and could not wait. His ego lorded it over him and demanded immediate attention: "Give me."

"And he [the father] divided unto them his living." The boy was not wise but his father was—to let him have his freedom to act a fool and not force him to be his father's fop at home. This was God's idea at Creation. Giving man free will was quite a gamble, but it is maturity's only hope. An embryo, overdue, dies. Man would have drowned in divinity in heaven, so God sent him away to mortality to school, to give him breathing space. Earth is a far country where man can find himself and find his need of God, firsthand.

This boy's father could have made him stay at home, say "Yes" to everything he said, and possessed him body and soul. But that would rob him of his manhood, produce a parasite. He defended his boy's right to be wrong, to make him able to be right one day, independently, and not because his father told him to. The time had come (to use Dr. Paul Popenoe's phrase) for "judicious neglect." The boy was already lost in selfishness, not ready now for good advice. He would have to find out the hard way. He must make a pilgrimage to find himself. It would be hell—and hell his hope.

"Not many days after the younger son gathered all together, and took his journey. . . ." It was a complete rejection of his home, his past, his father, his *self*. He wanted to get as far away as he could, to forget, to be free, to be as different as could be, to be somebody else. He would cancel the commandments. He wanted nothing of his father's faith—he sought a far country. "And there wasted his substance with riotous living." It was pandemonium. Shepherdless, he succumbed to the centrifugal pull of pleasure. Undisciplined, he bolted into a wilderness of savage flesh and forgot to say his prayers. His life became a stampede of self-indulgence, trampling, mutilating, exhausting everything fine and noble in him. Going far, he went too far, and exploded in one big futile brawl of desire.

"And when he had spent all, there arose a mighty famine in that land, and he began to be in want." Running away, he ran into something—the end of his string. Now he began to look the part he played. He dressed in rags and his address now plainly said: "Skid Row." His good times had gone, but it was still better, he kept telling himself, than being home. He began to taste dust in his mouth and a touch of age. He began to suffer and to starve, but he would not stop.

"And he went and joined himself to a citizen of that country, and he sent him into his fields to feed swine." It was worse than a dog's life—a pig's life—for a Jew, and a perfect picture of his predicament. "And he would fain have filled his belly with the husks that the swine did eat: and no man gave unto him." In his bull-headed attempt to get away from God he took himself prisoner. He had no friends, because he had never made friends with himself. What he thought were friends ran out with his money. And he was a "walking civil war" until he made his peace with God. He was dying, choking to death, in a tantrum of self-will, still screaming, "Give me." He would carry on to the bitter end what T. S. Eliot calls his "objection to the universe."

He "came to" in this helpless state. Hitting bottom was the beginning of him. He endured a delirium of doing what he wanted, then consciousness: "Why, this is hell." "My father's slaves live better than this." The last straw announces God. Life begins again in the disaster and despair that spells our need. Heaven builds its hopes on the defeat of man. It cannot help him until he discovers it and asks for help, as an alcoholic cannot win until he admits he's licked alone. This is the invitation God is waiting for before He can make a man. But it takes something more than saying "uncle." The boy not only gave up, he gave in. "I will arise and go to my father."

"When he came to himself. . . ." What a gracious expression—putting the best possible interpretation on our crimes. In this line, sin is sickness, something that happens when a man is not himself. It is out of character—a caricature. Jesus said, "When he came to himself," in such a way as to stamp no one in the status quo. He said it as if He were saying, promising, praying, some day every prodigal will return—ultimately this old rascal earth—"as it is in heaven."

"And the son said unto him, Father, I have sinned against heaven, and in thy sight, and am no more worthy to be called thy son." It was not merely the smart thing to do. He surrendered from sorrow, shame, and because he had grown sick of himself. His pride was broken and his confession burst out uncontrollably. It is sainthood's first and longest stride—when one becomes his own worst critic and the best of neighbors. The son saw his sin went deeper than his father and struck his father's God. "What have I done?" He stripped himself naked to the soul, and stood defenseless. "I have sinned against heaven."

"But when he was yet a great way off, his father saw him, and had compassion, and ran, and fell on his neck, and kissed him." The old man saw him first, and while the son was still a speck against the sky, swiftly covered all the distance pride and time had put between. Before the shivering, half-starved lad could finish his confession, he wrapped him in love's warm arms and kissed the rest of it away. He warned himself, "I'll catch it when I get home," but while he waited for his punishment, his father put a ring on his finger and shoes on his feet. He expected hard labor and at best a bite to eat, but he was shocked with happiness. He was wanted. And the reward for his repentance was to be the guest of honor. He thought his coming back would make a scene; he met instead a miracle of mercy. Someone had suffered more than the son, and had waited at the window for him all that time. It worked like magic. It filled the house with laughter and singing and sentenced all to happiness. A boy's guilt had painted doomsday black, but a father's forgiveness made it a holiday instead.

This scene is the supreme moment in all literature, the gem of His gospel—a God like that. Here the Author had in His head the greatest love story ever told. He would take time later to write it down indelibly in blood and glory. When our modern medicines and washing machines are as obsolete as bloodletting and the "Old Oaken Bucket"; when our space ships take their place on the shelf beside the steam engine and the buggywhip; when this planet waxes old like a garment, and the last sun sets, this story will still be young.

Jesus did not make up this story. It is true. Our God is like this father. And this lad? "This is your life" and mine. We may not be far away geographically, officially, nor far from the norm. But the big question this story raises is simply: "Where are you and I right now from God?" And until we come to ourselves, and go home, the Father of us all "standeth . . . within the shadows" watching for us, watching—and waiting.

Tragically, the story does not end here, but on a note of discord—the elder brother's fault. Coming home from work that day he "heard musick and dancing." When he learned why, he was enraged and would not have any part of it.

What was wrong with that? We have forgotten the way this Author felt and learned this story backwards. Men have become hardest on the sins of weakness and called the sins of pride defects. But Jesus called them every evil name He knew. He let the fallen woman, penitent, go in peace and poured on Pharisees all His wrath: "Fools, blind, leaders of the blind, blasphemers." "Tax-gatherers and prostitutes are entering the kingdom of God ahead of you." Doing the right thing for the wrong reason was not His idea of being a saint. The people who keep the rules are not God's people—necessarily. Keeping the letter of the law without its spirit is devil's work. Let the minister beware: "Everybody talkin' 'bout heaven ain't a'goin there." Pride, not prodigality, is chief of sinners in God's Book.

That is what was wrong with big brother: He stayed home and behaved himself—had been a model of decorum. Good boy? Only on the surface. Look beneath this veneer of propriety. He's a wolf in sheep's clothing. Why did he stay at home? Why, to save his skin. He knew which side his bread was buttered on. He is a veritable villain of decency, a very respectable criminal. "A good man in the worst sense of the word," as Mark Twain said. The boy is perfect—perfectly horrible—the perfect picture of the pride this Author hated most.

Look at him. He's not a pretty sight, close up. He's an ungrateful wretch. He might thank God his brother is safe, if only for his father's sake. He doesn't even say "hello," but storms: "You know how I have slaved for you all these years; I never once disobeyed your orders; and you never so much as gave me a kid . . . but now that this son of yours turns up"—he will not say "my little brother"—"after running through your money with his women. . . ." How does he know? Whatever this big boy had was less than he deserved. He never questioned his superiority, nor his brother's worthlessness. He was a self-righteous prig with no room for improvement. He could think of nothing to apologize

16

for—"I've never disobeyed." He was so proud that he was blinded to his pride.

And where was his heart? That is what God is looking for. It appears to be missing. The boy could not comprehend his father's grief when his brother left—"good riddance." And he couldn't imagine what there was to be happy about at his return —a headache. The more one sees of this older son the easier it is to understand why the young one left. He's not our choice for a fishing trip nor Kingdom's candidate. Who is the prodigal in this parable? The other came back. This one got lost at home.

The father does not argue with him. He addressed him tenderly: "My boy . . . you are always with me, and everything I have is yours." Then gently he reminded him: "How could we help celebrating this day? Your brother here was dead and has come back to life, was lost and is found." That is all that love can say and do. We do not know what the elder brother did. We know what he should have done—what we should do. No one shut him out of the banqueting hall. He locked himself out. The key he lost was love. And it will let us in as it would him.

"LISTEN to another parable. There was a householder who planted a vineyard, put a fence round it, dug a wine-vat inside it, and built a watchtower: then he leased it to vinedressers and went abroad. When the fruit-season was near, he sent his servants to the vinedressers to collect his fruit; but the vinedressers took his servants and flogged one, killed another, and stoned a third. Once more he sent some other servants, more than he had sent at first, and they did the same to them. Afterwards he sent them his son; 'They will respect my son,' he said. But when the vinedressers saw his son, they said to themselves, 'Here is the heir; come on, let us kill him and seize his inheritance!' So they took and threw him outside the vineyard and killed him. Now, when the owner of the vineyard comes, what will he do to these vinedressers?" They replied, "He will utterly destroy the wretches and lease the vineyard to other vinedressers, who will give him the fruits in their season."

MATTHEW 21:33-41 (also MARK 12:1-11, LUKE 20:9-18),

James Moffatt

✠

FOR it is as when a man, going into another country, called his own servants, and delivered unto them his goods. And unto one he gave five talents, to another two, to another one; to each according to his several ability; and he went on his journey. Straightway he that received the five talents went and traded with them, and made other five talents. In like manner he also that received the two gained other two. But he that received the one went away and digged in the earth, and hid his lord's money. Now after a long time the lord of those servants cometh, and maketh a reckoning with them. And he that received the five talents came and brought other five talents, saying, Lord,

thou *deliveredst unto me five talents: lo, I have gained other five talents. His lord said unto him, Well done, good and faithful servant: thou hast been faithful over a few things, I will set thee over many things: enter thou into the joy of thy lord. And he also that received the two talents came and said, Lord, thou deliveredst unto me two talents: lo, I have gained other two talents. His lord said unto him, Well done, good and faithful servant: thou hast been faithful over a few things, I will set thee over many things: enter thou into the joy of thy lord. And he also that had received the one talent came and said, Lord, I knew thee that thou art a hard man, reaping where thou didst not sow, and gathering where thou didst not scatter; and I was afraid, and went away and hid thy talent in the earth: lo, thou hast thine own. But his lord answered and said unto him, Thou wicked and slothful servant, thou knewest that I reap where I sowed not, and gather where I did not scatter; thou oughtest therefore to have put my money to the bankers, and at my coming I should have received back mine own with interest. Take ye away therefore the talent from him, and give it unto him that hath the ten talents. For unto every one that hath shall be given, and he shall have abundance: but from him that hath not, even that which he hath shall be taken away. And cast ye out the unprofitable servant into the outer darkness: there shall be the weeping and the gnashing of teeth.*
MATTHEW 25:14-30 (also LUKE 19:11-27),

American Standard Version

✠

T HEN *shall the kingdom of heaven be likened unto ten virgins, who took their lamps, and went forth to meet the bridegroom. And five of them were foolish, and five were wise. For the foolish, when they took their lamps, took no oil with them: but the wise took oil in their vessels with their lamps. Now while the bridegroom tarried, they all slumbered and slept. But at midnight there is a cry, Behold, the bridegroom! Come ye forth to meet him. Then all those virgins arose, and trimmed their lamps. And the foolish said unto the wise, Give us of your oil; for our lamps are going out. But the wise answered, saying, Peradventure there will not be enough for us and you: go ye rather to them that sell, and buy for yourselves. And while they went away to buy, the bridegroom came; and they that were ready went in with him to the marriage feast: and the door was shut. Afterward came also the other virgins, saying, Lord, Lord, open to us. But he answered and said, Verily I say unto you, I know you not. Watch therefore, for ye know not the day nor the hour.*

MATTHEW 25:1-13, American Standard Version

2

The Rebellious Tenants
The Talents
The Wise and Foolish Girls

THIS GOD TO whom we are introduced in the Testament is actually our Father. Christ identifies Him as available, understanding, tender, yet firm, informed, and capable. And there is one forgotten finishing touch to His Fatherhood Christ puts into these three parables. God has gone away for awhile. He has the Kingdom and the power, and is definitely within hearing and helping distance, but He keeps His distance. He is earth's Chief Executive, but He is not operating from earth, but to it—from His Capitol in heaven. His seat at the head of our table is somehow empty. However, He is expected—and we pray for that expectation in the Lord's Prayer and our Lord preached that expectation in these parables of a returning Lord and Master.

God has not deserted, but carried out a strategic retreat to provide man an opportunity to prove His stewardship. God knows when to let growing boys be. He doesn't miss a thing, but He won't meddle. He is always there when you need Him, but He will never let His goodness get in the way of what is good for us. God couldn't make men of us underfoot in our Father's house. Like a wise Father He has put some time and space between us. Life is our time of trial and temptation. Time is an interval when we are to a certain extent on our own. We are not isolated, but given breathing space.

Man is not automatically hauled into heaven by the compelling act of Creation. God makes heaven man's decision. We have not been thrust into a nursery next to the Throne Room but forced into freedom. We are under the eye but not the thumb of God; we are not treated like helpless kindergartners but as responsible adolescents. This magnificent Absentee Landlord Image declares we are cut from the Almighty's apron strings, nudged from the nest, urged to try our own wings on a downstage planet and be ready when He comes back. "Standeth God within the shadows" to give man his shining opportunity to be himself.

The first parable tells about some tenants who took things into their own hands as soon as the Landlord left, and when the Landlord sent servants to collect the rent the tenants beat them. "But afterward he sent unto them his son, saying they will reverence my son. But they (renters) when they saw the son, said among themselves, this is the heir; come let us kill him, and take his inheritance. And they . . . killed him."

This skit has caught man red-handed in his most characteristic crime—playing God. While God's back is turned, or He has momentarily left the room, man has rebelled and taken over the class himself. The parable's picture is brutally honest. Earth gives man his chance to prepare his lessons, invest his talents and get ready for the examination. But what has he done? He has exploited this study hall to put his own feet under the Teacher's desk. And in the laboratory, in open defiance of His text, he has mixed the materials to his own advantage to feather what he has the nerve to call his own nest. And if he can't get his own way he threatens to blow up the schoolhouse with an atomic concoction.

With infinite patience the Almighty has sent prophet after prophet to His property to remind them of their rent. But the people there stoned every one of them. Then in the fullness of time He sent His Son, saying, "Surely, they will reverence him," but they killed Him. It takes no genius to observe that the mutiny that did away with Him continues. George Bernard Shaw believed to his death that the martyrdom of Joan of Arc is a burning issue—that the Cross is not a relic at all, but exactly what modern man does to Christ in his own inimitable way.

Notice our own engagement in this desperate cheat. How many

men act like trustees with their "time, talents, possessions"? Modern living seems a mad scramble for "Squatter's Rights," without the slightest regard for the One who made us and left us here. Life behaves as a huge recess. We don't have to answer to anyone except "they." No one supposes he is subject to some superior audit. How many bind up the scattered pages of their daily activities into a supreme record of stewardship? The average man's plans are ultimately pension plans. Perhaps he divides up his estate fairly for his family in his will. But he acts as if he were dividing up "mine" instead of "thine." Bryant's word has been erased, "So live, that when thy summons comes to join the innumerable caravan. . . ."

According to this parable this is the time-honored pattern of human behavior. And this is what the Bible means by living in sin. A man may be decent, honest, hardworking, ambitious and faithful—but so was Lucifer. The key to his fall was that he ignored God and fought to take away God's inalienable rights.

The parable closes with a question and answer. The question is: "When the Lord of the Vineyard shall come, what will he do to these renters?" And the answer: "He will miserably destroy those miserable men, and will let the vineyard out unto other (renters) who shall render him the fruit of their seasons." The point of the parable is that God will return and justice will be done.

This does not mean God is not merciful or fair. It does mean He is businesslike. He has placed us here in positions of trust and sometime He will return and have a right to expect something of us. He has given us fair warning again and again! This life is not a farce, nor all volleying for serve—it is a game in earnest. Someone who knows what we can do is keeping score and "The night cometh, when no man can work." There is too much suffering and strain in life to say He lied this time. Any honest estimate will confirm the gospel's impression that our life is leading up to something, Someone, when we shall have to face up to what we've done and didn't get away with; and if on that day wrongs are to be righted and the crooked

23

made straight, we shall have to be straightened out. Some day we must at last look Him in the eye. Who says that ordeal will not be painful?

The next parable on the talents lights up Judgment's individual character. Before the Landlord left this time he gave to one "five talents, to another two, to another one, each according to his several ability." All men are created unequal in God's country in everything except legal rights.

God will not grade on the curve or by some arbitrary standard. Each man will be matched against his own ability and opportunity. When this Landlord returns Luke writes: "And that servant who knew his master's will, but did not make ready or act according to his will, shall receive a severe beating. But he who did not know . . . shall receive a light beating." God is going to expect more from Chicago than the Congo. The flat rate practice is foreign to Christianity. The Landlord will settle each case separately. Each man will be weighed, not as he compares with Jones, but with his own model self.

And God is going to be hardest of all on the best. This will bring small consolation to the man who thinks he is better than other men. Let the Pharisee beware—the bar will be raised for the morally superior. Every contestant must come across with thoughts, words, and deeds, worthy of the Christian advantages he has had. In this proportionate light Hitler may fare better in hell than some overprivileged Presbyterian. God will be most severe with those of us who call ourselves Christian. The people who need to look out, as Amos cried long ago, are not the lost so much as the Chosen. "You only have I known of all the families of the earth," saith the Lord, "therefore I will visit upon you all your iniquities." After teaching in the towns of Chorazin and Bethsaida without any success, Jesus had this to say on the same subject. "But I say unto you that it shall be more tolerable in that day for Sodom than for (this) city. Woe to you, Chorazin! woe to you, Bethsaida! for if the mighty works done in you had been done in Tyre and Sidon, they would have repented long ago in sackcloth and ashes. But I tell you, it shall be more tolerable on the day of judgment for Tyre and Sidon than for you." In the Day of Judgment it may be easier for the Almighty to be merciful to the communists in Russia than to those of us who live "in freedom's holy light." "To whom much is given, of him much will be required."

In fact, you and I are going to be blamed for some things our neighbors did. It is this disturbing insight that Dostoevski drives home through his Saint Father Zossima. That good Priest informs Alyosha that a Christian takes on tremendous responsibility for his neighbors. "The criminal in your community may be less guilty for his crime than you—his Christian neighbor. For you could have been a light to the evildoer, yet you were not, for the man remained beside you in darkness. Had you been the kind of example you ought to have been and shone your lantern on that lost man's path, perhaps he might not have stumbled into murder. If you had loved your neighbor as yourself and lavished upon him some of the care you generously lavish upon yourself—shared some of the warmth God has privileged you to possess—that murderer might have been changed in time."

The water gets deep here, but this is the stand Christ took on the Cross as in the parable. Some shoulders are broader and should carry other's overload. Some eyes see farther and are expected to guide the nearsighted. Some hearts are bigger and are meant to transfuse the Christian spirit into lives unable to pump enough for themselves. There was once a Man who it is said never sinned; and it was this innocent Man who undertook to pay for the sins of the whole world. "To whom much is given, of him much will be required."

But we have looked long enough at the dark side of God's homecoming. And while we will get justice, God will come back dressed as a Bridegroom, not a Judge, to the tune of a wedding march, not a funeral dirge. This is the bright Kodachrome we get in the parable of the wise and foolish girls. The scene on that great day will not take place in some courtroom, but in a banquet hall. The Master will be in His best mood eager to believe the best. We are not subpoenaed to our trial and execution but invited to a celebration. There will be laughter and hearts will be light.

This sketch sharpens another feature of God's return: the element of surprise. No one knows when He is coming back in any of these three parables, but in this one the drama is heightened because the bridegroom is delayed. When will God come back to us? We only know when He does it will sweep us off our feet and take our breath away. "Watch ye therefore . . . at even, or at midnight, or at the cockcrowing, or in the morning." God is full of surprises. It is one of His outstanding characteristics. The thing happened to the ten young maids when they were fast asleep. "There was a cry at midnight."

This last scene gives us a good idea of God's benchside manner. All these girls were sleeping. Nothing wrong with that. But the emergency caught five out of oil for their lamps. This situation more nearly describes the action on Judgment Day: Not as something God is going to do to us—but as something we didn't do. "Even so it is not the will of your Father which is in heaven, that one of these little ones should perish," and He will be eagerly expecting and be ready for us all. The larger question is: "Will we be ready?"

The five foolish girls ran in vain to the wise to borrow oil. Not because the wise aren't generous. This is a parable, not an allegory. This is the parable's way of saying you can't lend wisdom on the spur of the moment. No matter how much the five wise wanted and were willing to sacrifice for the foolish, there is a limit to how much can be done for the foolish at the last minute. Wisdom is not marketable. Instant wisdom has not been developed. In a crisis the wise are sometimes resented because they can't transfer their character to some shallow, giddy creature; she has no place where it will stick. The superficial cannot pin the blame on God or good people for being excluded. The point is they are in no position to accept; they have no place to put such a deep experience. They are completely undressed for glory—and now it's too late. The bridegroom did not shut the door in their faces. They had locked themselves out long ago.

Christianity does not brace us to face the music but enlarges us to appreciate it. The happy fact is that we have all been invited to a wedding. None of us knows exactly when it will take place. But we know that we will have to secure oil now to be ready for any such emergency of joy. We will have to think about it now and get in the right frame of mind and heart now in order to be in the right mood for that midnight when we hear "a bridegroom's cry of joy."

'THE kingdom of Heaven is like this. There was once a landowner who went out early one morning to hire labourers for his vineyard; and after agreeing to pay them the usual day's wage he sent them off to work. Going out three hours later he saw some more men standing idle in the market-place. "Go and join the others in the vineyard," he said, "and I will pay you a fair wage"; so off they went. At noon he went out again, and at three in the afternoon, and made the same arrangement as before. An hour before sunset he went out and found another group standing there; so he said to them, "Why are you standing about like this all day with nothing to do?" "Because no one has hired us," they replied; so he told them, "Go and join the others in the vineyard." When evening fell, the owner of the vineyard said to his steward, "Call the labourers and give them their pay, beginning with those who came last and ending with the first." Those who had started work an hour before sunset came forward, and were paid the full day's wage. When it was the turn of the men who had come first, they expected something extra, but were paid the same amount as the others. As they took it, they grumbled at their employer: "These latecomers have done only one hour's work, yet you have put them on a level with us, who have sweated the whole day long in the blazing sun!" The owner turned to one of them and said, "My friend, I am not being unfair to you. You agreed on the usual wage for the day, did you not? Take your pay and go home. I choose to pay the last man the same as you. Surely I am free to do what I like with my own money. Why be jealous because I am kind?" Thus will the last be first, and the first last.'

MATTHEW 20:1-16, New English Bible

3

The Controversial Employer

AFTER THE RICH young ruler turned Him down, Jesus came to this pessimistic conclusion: "It is easier for a camel to go through the eye of a needle than for a rich man to enter the Kingdom of God." At this point He was not talking exclusively to Astor or Rockefeller, but as usual to you and me. For to this homeless Near Eastern Man anyone who has a home, two pairs of shoes, and three full meals a day has "great possessions." His disciples saw it was a sweeping statement for they all cried out at once: "Who then can be saved?" He replied: "With men this is impossible, but with God all things are possible." Prosperity is a precarious blessing, and unless a man makes the necessary religious arrangements to police possessions in second place they will eventually sneak in and steal his soul. Comfort can cause drowsiness and laying a little aside for a rainy day can become a mushrooming business. So Jesus issued the warning to make us see we had better pray: "So help me God."

What the rich were in for made the disciples wonder what they were going to get out of all they had given up. So Peter tried to pry: "Lo, we have left everything and followed you. What then shall we have?" Peter would live to regret that question. For the words were hard as this old world and must have hurt the Teacher. But they were honest and had to be answered. Yes, Jesus reassured him, they would all be rewarded royally, but there was something radically wrong with ever worrying about it or working for it. "Many that are first," He said, "will be last, and the last first." But He saw that statement was not a satisfactory explanation so it reminded Him of a story—a story that seems so strange we've tried to avoid it and made it the wallflower of the parables. But that is because we have never really met its meaning.

"The kingdom of heaven is like a householder who went out early in the morning to hire laborers for his vineyard." He found a few who agreed to work for a price and got them started. About nine o'clock in the morning he saw some more unemployed men hopefully standing around downtown and put them to work, promising to pay whatever was right. He went out at noon and also in the middle of the afternoon and did the same thing. Then at the eleventh hour, or at about five o'clock, he noticed others still waiting for work, so he also gave them a job and they went up willingly to his plantation.

This parable is not a lecture on economics, although it shows Jesus was not afraid of the touchy question of capital and labor. And one can see through this story to Christ's sympathy for men out of work. And this capitalist is an example to any corporation. He not only needs men, but Dr. A. B. Bruce believes he likes men as much as profit. What else prompted him to hire them so close to quitting time if not pity?

So far there is nothing eccentric about this story, but this land-lord is a hero and he is a character. And if one cannot see it in the way he hires men, it grows quite clear in the way he pays them off. When the stars came out, for that was the factory whistle in those days, he directed his steward to settle up with them. He fooled everyone. The men who were hired last were paid first. Furthermore, he paid them for a full day's work. Then he called up each gang in the reverse order of their engagement and paid them all the same amount. "Now when the first came they thought they would receive more, but each of them also received a denarius."

"And on receiving it, they grumbled at the householder, saying, 'These last worked only one hour, and you have made them equal to us who have borne the burden of the day and the scorching heat.' " That expresses our sentiments exactly. It does not seem fair for those who had put in a twelve-hour day to get no more than those last-minute men. But this story does not want to call attention to itself, but to life itself. And this house-holder is not speaking for capital but for God when he says in self-defense: "Friend, I am doing you no wrong; did you not agree with me for a denarius? Take what belongs to you, and go. . . . Am I not allowed to do what I choose with what belongs to me? Or do you begrudge my generosity?" Even as an employer he kept his part of the bargain. But this parable is trying to answer Peter's question, "What are we going to get out of the good life?" And this story is saying the great Landowner has every right to reward men any way He wishes. That is *His* business. Who are we to question Him about heaven's pay scale? He does not have to answer to us. "Neither are your ways my ways, saith the Lord." He is inscrutable and "past finding out." He is not a piece of transparent plastic or He would not be God. Capital cannot do anything it likes with labor, but God can do as He pleases with man and not be called on the carpet for it. Did Jesus stop here to say: "Do you hear this Peter?" "Can everyone hear me?"

What else is this strange story saying? It is loaded with meaning, particularly for anyone who calls himself a friend of Christ, and the fact that He delivered it to His disciples on the eve of His last journey emphasizes it.

It reveals that whatever God gives is unmerited grace. Man is head over heels in God's debt and for any man to dare bill Almighty God for every little bit of goodness he does down here is the height of the ridiculous. The men who did the most did no more than their fair share. And here they had the sacred honor of being God's servant first and longest. Why did they not thrill to the blessing of being most valuable to Him? They had the coveted opportunity and they complained. And they were paid as promised for this holy privilege. Why were they worrying about more reward when all that time they had the rich pleasure of His company and the sweet content of being useful? Their pay was bonus to that bliss. God is far more generous to the saints than they deserve and they are the first to say so, but these men's noses were in the air, stuck in someone else's business. It would be almost impossible for men with such a high opinion of themselves ever to say "thank you." How could they ever know the feeling of gratitude if they felt they had earned every solid penny of their lives, that they owed their prosperity to themselves? They would never know how to give back anything out of appreciation or how to be happy over any latecomer's legacy.

This story is saying, too, that God passes out the same salvation to us all. Heaven is heaven no matter who goes there or when. When a man comes to himself, whether it is as a prodigal son or on his deathbed, he goes home to the same Father. The penitent thief on the cross got as big a piece of paradise as innocent Joan of Arc. His penalty was his past—the time he put in hell while away in the far country.

Those "early birds" sound very much like the prodigal son's elder brother, working for his father, putting up a good front of faithfulness, but doing it all with an ulterior motive, to get special privileges. He was doing what his father said, not for his father's sake, but to get the farm. He didn't care for his father or his brother. He built a good reputation because he knew that was the smart way to hog earth and heaven too. These first men in the field that day were committing this same abominable sin of doing the right things for the wrong reason—being good not because God said to, and they loved to, but with their beady eyes on the prize. Goodness in them was egotistical and so it was the devil's work.

For goodness is not a strategy, a clever conspiracy to break into heaven. Paradise is not our pay for earthwork, "lest any man should boast." If it is goodness it is done for love of God and man, for its own sake, because it cannot be helped—it is the fruit of kindness, overpayment in itself. It is something that keeps its hands off heaven as not its property but left up to God to give in His own way, just as is the blessed opportunity to serve Him here.

The spiritually privileged had better watch out. This is a warning to calculating pulpiteers and crafty churchgoers. If some mercenary motive drives them to church and charity they will lose the race for heaven to the harlots and the bums. The most spotless life doesn't mean a thing to God unless the heart is right. God penalizes good conduct if done for selfish reasons, for "many that are first will be last."

The men who went to work last in this story were not at fault for being late. Unemployment can mean laziness, but here it means hard times. These men were robbed of their place in the sun by circumstances beyond their control. Heaven pays a man back for earth's shortchange in opportunities. But it is certainly clear from the lightning look we get on life by this that God pays not on the basis of volume of work we have accomplished, but on the spirit in which we did what we could. Men will be paid not for what they did, so much as for what they would have done if they had had the chance—and that shows by the way they acted in the little time life allowed them on the field. Dr. Bruce sees God's weakness for the humble showing here. For the first men bargained for their wages, but the last went right to work without a murmuring word about what they were worth.

What do you see in this compelling masterpiece? It is at least somehow a mural of the last great day. Many who have worked hard, heartlessly, who have done what was expected of them, may not receive what they expect. Most of the grumbling over grades in the next world may come, not from the ones we have said were "no good" here, but from men who were good for nothing but what they could get out of it. And others who have done pitifully little, but not through any fault of their own, may be stunned by His generosity. For as blind Milton saw in this holy light, "They also serve who only stand and wait."

Do not despair. For if this story is a warning to the distinguished, it is an encouragement to those "born to blush unseen." It does not matter if a man has little to show to the naked eye for this life. One day, after the rich men had poured all their impressive tithes in the treasury, "a poor widow put in two copper coins. And he said . . . this poor widow has put in more than all of them"; for she had tried hard, loved much, and asked for nothing but a little mercy. "But many that are first will be last, and the last first."

THEN he said to them, "Suppose one of you has a friend, and you go to him at midnight and say to him, 'Friend, let me have three loaves; for a friend of mine travelling has come to my house and I have nothing to set before him.' And suppose he answers from the inside, 'Don't bother me; the door is locked by this time, and my children are in bed with me. I can't get up and give you anything.' I tell you, though he will not get up and give you anything because you are a friend of his, he will at least rise and give you whatever you want, because you persist. So I tell you, ask and the gift will be yours, seek and you will find, knock and the door will open to you; for everyone who asks receives, the seeker finds, the door is opened to anyone who knocks. What father among you, if asked by his son for a loaf, will hand him a stone?—or, if asked for a fish, will hand him a serpent instead of a fish?—or, if asked for an egg, will he hand him a scorpion? Well, if for all your evil you know to give your children what is good, how much more will your Father give the holy Spirit from heaven to those who ask him?"

LUKE 11:5-13, James Moffatt

✠

AND he told them a parable, to the effect that they ought always to pray and not lose heart. He said, "In a certain city there was a judge who neither feared God nor regarded man; and there was a widow in that city who kept coming to him and saying, 'Vindicate me against my adversary.' For a while he refused; but afterward he said to himself, 'Though I neither fear God nor regard man, yet because this widow bothers me, I will vindicate her, or she will wear me out by her continual coming.'" And the Lord said, "Hear what the unrighteous judge says. And will not

35

God vindicate his elect, who cry to him day and night? Will he delay long over them? I tell you, he will vindicate them speedily. Nevertheless, when the Son of man comes, will he find faith on earth?"

LUKE 18:1-8, Revised Standard Version

4

A Friend Who Got Up at Midnight
The Persistent Widow

THIS IS NOT the first time Jesus talked about prayer to His disciples. They had said, "Lord, teach us to pray," before, and He had given them His prayer to show them how. This assignment sounds like the second lesson—as if they had tried His prayer at home and returned to report, "It won't work." And now to help them with their homework, or to give them more, He made up two more parables "to the effect that they ought always to pray and not lose heart."

One time a man had unexpected company arrive very late at night, and they caught him without a bite to eat in the house. In those days a host had to give his guests something to eat before bed, so this one ran to his friend's house and banged on the door to borrow bread. An unfriendly voice came from the darkened bedroom: "Do not bother me. The door is shut for the night; my children and I have gone to bed." But the embarrassed host kept up the racket. So the disgruntled fellow got up at midnight to give his neighbor whatever he wanted, not out of friendship, but to get rid of him.

Now if some grouchy sleepyhead would answer a midnight knock just to get some peace, how much more eagerly will a good God open the door to His petitioners to supply their more desperate needs out of His vast larder? "Is there a father among you who will offer his son a snake when he asks for a fish, or a scorpion when he asks for an egg? If you, then, bad as you are, know how to give your children what is good for them, how much more will the heavenly Father. . . ."

The answer does not clear up all our questions, but it makes a compelling point. We are weak, yet strong enough to bring home the bacon and send our sons through school. Consider the God of strength, who has leased us ours; are we not pikers in comparison to the great Provider? Are we so blind, so ego struck, as to believe we can do more for ours than He for His? Before you give up praying, think of the precious time you are able to play Santa Claus to your son. You are no Croesus, yet you are rich enough to fill his Christmas stockings with his wishes and hear and answer his birthday prayers. Have you led him to think you can outdo the father's Father? We are selfish, but if our son were crying for bread, we would beg or steal or starve ourselves before he starved. Yet surely the supreme sacrifice we make for our children is midget size beside the mighty offering of the King of Heaven to any child who cares to ask. We are only human yet would go to any length, but He is divine—look upon His Cross! What ever made us think we could beat God at His business of goodness? Before you throw His prayer away, just look at what mothers and fathers have gone through to make the prayers of their boys and girls come true, and don't forget: "They are but broken lights of Thee, and Thou O Lord art more than they." Our sons may need to waken us to save them from the fire, but "He that keepeth Israel shall neither slumber nor sleep." "My son, just see all I've done for you," and yet, "No one is good but God alone." Perhaps our best present to our son is to prepare him for the time when he can no longer write home, and protect him now from such a limited concept of goodness as our poor deeds describe. So let these earthly fathers' flickering stabs at love lift all our prayers to the unfailing light of Him above.

Jesus left another clue to God in this anecdote. God is not a principle; He is personal. Now God is no hibernating neighbor sky-high—that figure is used not to show what God is like but to sharpen the contrast. And just because God is personal does not mean He is anthropomorphic. It does mean He is not mechanical—but at least like a good father, though far more. Jesus used people to describe God, because He is more like the best we can see in people than anything else we can think of. The most that you and I can say about God in one word now is

—Jesus. And the little bit of God that Jesus could show us in His stories is lifted from the daily lives of men.

Now that story still has something more to say, but He told a second to put it another way. There was once a hard-boiled judge who wasn't afraid of God or anyone else. Now a destitute widow came to him for help, and of course, he turned her down flat. But she kept on coming, until finally the judge said he would help her—not because her cause was just, nor because his heart melted, but simply, as he said, "This widow is so great a nuisance that I will see her righted before she wears me out. . . ." Then Jesus drove home the point: If a cruel judge would hear a persistent widow's plea, will not a merciful God take care of those who cry to Him day and night?

This story shouts, as the first suggests, that prayer isn't any good unless it is persistent. God won't give us what we want the first time we ask for it—what Robert Collyer called: "The determination of heaven not to hear what we are not determined that heaven shall hear." God won't read the third class mail nor pay any attention to the casual "off the cuff" asides, the fresh remarks of juke boxes, nor listen to the leftovers we leave Him at the fag end of the day. The flashily said "God love you's" with which some ministers tastelessly sprinkle their parish, the ritual slang, the fresh remarks the mob makes as it breaks into the cathedral each week, undressed for church inside, irreverently chattering to God about those unimportant things they know He'll approve if He should overhear—these blurbs are beneath His interest. Those who take prayer so lightly they can't remember what it was they meant to pray for and never pray for the same thing two weeks in a row, who assume one mention is enough, at least to be mad about if He doesn't answer within the hour, make prayer a pity.

According to this parable, prayer is more than this. God is sales resistant to the random request. Prayer demands determination, and patience. When Jacob met the Angel, he did not merely pass the time of day, he wrestled with him. It was not sport. "I will not let thee go, except thou bless me." Paul talked to God about his "thorn," not in passing but eagerly, fervently, not once but three times before he was blessed. The Master of prayer Himself did not dash off His vespers, but prayed all night, night after night, and in Gethsemane went over that awful decision again and again, and finally flung Himself face down and prayed so earnestly that those who saw it said, "His sweat was as it were great drops of blood falling down to the ground." To attract the notice of the Almighty, prayer must have something of the insistence, the perseverence, the intensity, of the undiscouraged host who kept banging away at his neighbor's door at night, or the undaunted widow who kept pestering the tough old judge with her problem and wouldn't give up until he gave in.

Why? Why the crowded waiting room—the tubs full of tears before God hears? Why the delay? Celestial red tape? Is God overworked, understaffed, cruel? Or could the bottleneck be us —prayer's answer postponed for our sake? We say it is.

First, to show us who's God. If our answer does not pop out as promptly as our fortune stub when we step on the scales, that proves, not God's indifference, impotence, but His power—He's our Father not our slave to come when our hands are folded as if a finger snapped. The delay is our education in humility. The idea that God knows and we don't sinks in slowly. Quick results fool us into believing we brought them all by ourselves. It takes time to tell it is from God and not manufactured. "But they that wait upon the Lord . . ." become a little less sure of themselves, a little less smug. They are blessed with the meek.

And secondly, God's deliberateness prevents the wrong prayer from getting anywhere. Looking back we are grateful He didn't always give us what we asked for first. We shall be ashamed of some of today's prayers, tomorrow. Some won't bear repeating in that light. Practice makes perfect, polishes off the pagan edges, shifts the weight away from us. The longer we pray for Christ's sake, the less we are likely to pray unworthily. The sham, the dirty, sub-Christian requests, slip away as we say our prayers near the Cross. Galileo visited the tomb of St. Anthony intending to ask for money for himself, health for his children, and old age for his mother, but standing there in the inspiration of that Saint's sacrifice, he found himself saying, "I beg you, St. Anthony, to plead with Jesus Christ for me that He should enlighten my mind and let me invent something very great to further human knowledge." I shall not soon forget some-one else who said so short a time ago that he would like to say a prayer. I know he had his heart set on something else, at first, but in the Presence, shaped by suffering, he was at last deeply moved by the goodness of God to ask for permission to speak a thanks. The wait, the interminable, terrible, awful wait, wrung from him the prayer that made heaven rain with blessing.

God holds back also until we pray with passion—until all the yawns are gone and the sleepy, halfhearted hopes and dreams become burning desires. Prayer is only play until it is intense, relentless. Prayer can't bring peace nor compete with evil until we want peace more than anything else in the world. The kingdom is no scheme to "get rich quick," and that makes us want it all the more. "Home is dearer when the journey's long." He makes heaven most precious by saving it for the last, for those who won't give up.

But God will answer. Prayer takes more than we've been putting into it. But no honest, earnest, prayer will be lost. Not even a dead-tired neighbor nor a hard-boiled judge can resist determined petition. How much less our Father who is in heaven.

THEN Jesus addressed him. "Simon," he said, "I have something to say to you." "Speak, teacher," he said. "There was a moneylender who had two debtors; one owed him fifty pounds, the other five. As they were unable to pay, he freely forgave them both. Tell me, now, which of them will love him most?" "I suppose," said Simon, "the man who had most forgiven." "Quite right," he said. Then turning to the woman he said to Simon, "You see this woman? When I came into your house, you never gave me water for my feet, while she has wet my feet with her tears and wiped them with her hair; you never gave me a kiss, while ever since she came in she has kept pressing kisses on my feet; you never anointed my head with oil, while she has anointed my feet with perfume. Therefore I tell you, many as her sins are, they are forgiven, for her love is great; whereas he to whom little is forgiven has but little love." And he said to her, "Your sins are forgiven."

LUKE 7:40-49, James Moffatt

✛

THEN Peter came up and asked him, 'Lord, how often am I to forgive my brother if he goes on wronging me? As many as seven times?' Jesus replied, 'I do not say seven times; I say seventy times seven.

'The kingdom of Heaven, therefore, should be thought of in this way: There was once a king who decided to settle accounts with the men who served him. At the outset there appeared before him a man whose debt ran into millions. Since he had no means of paying, his master ordered him to be sold to meet the debt, with his wife, his children, and everything he had. The man fell prostrate at his master's feet. "Be patient with me," he said, "and I will pay in full"; and the master was so moved

43

with pity that he let the man go and remitted the debt. But no sooner had the man gone out than he met a fellow-servant who owed him a few pounds; and catching hold of him he gripped him by the throat and said, "Pay me what you owe." The man fell at his fellow-servant's feet, and begged him, "Be patient with me, and I will pay you"; but he refused, and had him jailed until he should pay the debt. The other servants were deeply distressed when they saw what had happened, and they went to their master and told him the whole story. He accordingly sent for the man. "You scoundrel!" he said to him; "I remitted the whole of your debt when you appealed to me; were you not bound to show your fellow-servant the same pity as I showed to you?" And so angry was the master that he condemned the man to torture until he should pay the debt in full. And that is how my heavenly Father will deal with you, unless you each forgive your brother from your hearts.'

MATTHEW 18:21-35, New English Bible

5

Two Debtors
Two Creditors

WE SAY, "Forgive us our debts as we forgive" too often, and are too sure of ourselves to deserve it. We act as if we know all about forgiveness and didn't owe any or need a bit. If this is so, we have done something very foolish, and forgotten almost all He ever said on the subject. Forgiveness is free but it's *not* free and easy. His course on forgiveness is the most advanced He had to offer—in fact the hardest on the teacher. His findings were so upsetting, so in conflict with traditional ethical practice, so imperiously demanding on anyone's time and moral energy, it is hard to see how we can say, "I'm sorry," and "Forget it," so casually. Forgiveness made the disciples hold up their hands in consternation. So before Jesus acted it all out in the last act, He tried to put it into moving words in two very businesslike parables.

The very idea of forgiveness was quickly buried, as He was too, under thick layers of misunderstanding, tightly locked with a huge rock of fear, and later with a mental block of compromise. This way these two parables are explained away. Someone is always supposed to say: "You know how He always exaggerated in that Oriental way of His." And these two stories are just a little questionable for our conservative stage. Some wish He hadn't said them; some don't wish to be seen with them. Let us look quickly just now and run. That is all anyone has ever done. Is that true? By any chance can someone stay? Oh, that will never do, unless they are true, and we are not afraid. Let us listen to Him for once, just this once, and not for all.

One night Simon the Pharisee had Jesus over for dinner. One gets the impression, despite Simon's seemingly halfhearted invitation, that Jesus was delighted to come. Jesus never wasted

His time with anyone. He put everything He had into everything He did and the results were unbelievable. And He took this cool reception and made it into a memorable evening too. In our effort to make Him seem so calm and reasonable, we forget what a bombshell He was to respectable society then. If He had had a Boswell we never would have believed him. It would not take many more nights like this to nail Him to the scaffold.

Simon is the perfect "straight man" for the suspense that builds up. While they were eating dinner something completely unrehearsed and totally unexpected broke the ice of this rigidly Puritan household. In from the streets stepped a fallen woman. She was one of those who had fallen more than once—or twice. It was her whole life. Simon was speechless. Only an Adams in Victorian Boston could grasp his horror. The dwellings in those days opened off the street and strangers could come and go and sit and talk as long as they kept their place in the seat along the outside wall. But no prostitute would dare do such a thing.

Before Simon recovered from the shock of her entrance, she proceeded to create what to him was a scene, but it seemed beautiful to Christ. She brought in an alabaster box, and suddenly, standing there behind Christ, she broke down in tears. This Man was so different from the others. His eyes were kind and clear of lust. She had never been treated like that before. And it made her memories more than she could stand. She took down her hair to hide the red-eyed shame. This would be a night she would not have to forget and one that would help her forget the others. She knew it was not wrong, for it was holy where she washed His feet with kisses and dried them with her hair.

Simon tapped his foot all through this part of the Scripture. The way this Jesus was taking it confirmed his suspicions. If Simon was scandalized by Mary, he was disgusted with his guest: "He said to himself, 'if this man were a prophet, he would

46

have known who and what sort of woman this is who is touching him.' " Jesus read his mind and set Simon straight.

Simon had not rolled out the red carpet for Christ in the first place. The invitation had come out of a dab of curiosity and a pinch of condescension. Jesus did not mind that, but this hostility to Mary was too much. Here she was, doing the honors Simon had insultingly omitted; still Simon sneered. Jesus, as usual taking the side of the underdog, came swiftly to her rescue.

"Simon, I have something to say to you." The announcement made Simon speak up with respect, "What is it Teacher?" Everyone knows how good-hearted Jesus was, but to say He was kind means to some people that He was an innocuous well-wisher. Mary could not have found a more talented trial lawyer anywhere in any time. Kindness to this Man meant using His head and hard work. For in a few minutes He had developed a case for her defense that Socrates himself could not match. It was this harmless-looking little parable lying here in Luke. "A certain creditor had two debtors. The one owed 500 denari, and the other fifty. When they could not pay, he forgave them both. Now which of them will love him more?" It was a brilliant stroke. Jesus did not attack Simon. He threw him off guard with a question, then let him hang himself. "Which will love him more?" And Simon had to admit, much as he didn't like it, "The one, I suppose, to whom he forgave more." One of the most exciting ideas the world has ever had was born right then in the mouth of Simon the Pharisee.

This does not mean that Jesus took Mary's sin lightly. This story isn't recommending sin so God has more to pardon and man more reason to love Him. The devil tempted Jesus to do just that, once. But He didn't have to jump from a high tower to feel God's love. "Thou shalt not tempt the Lord thy God." Mary's past was a painful tragedy. She didn't need to do all that to see how far God would go for her. Jesus is commending Mary's *consciousness* of sin, not her sin. The healthy thing about Mary is her guilt feelings which made her eligible for her discovery at the feet of Christ. She saw what a King's helping of mercy it took to save her life and it broke her heart with thanks. Which came first, forgiveness or love? Who knows? Love and forgiveness are never very far apart. Love has eyes that can see in the dark. Love has feelings. It suffers from sin like nothing else. And love longs to get back to Him who first loved us. Love reacts violently to sin. Only goodness agrees with love. Sooner or later love learns that it is extremely sensitive to the slightest wish of God.

Simon, orthodox as he is, doesn't really care for God—would not cry if God died. Why? First, he doesn't know about the fall—doesn't know there is anything wrong with man. "For all have sinned and come short of the glory . . ." is news to him. Simon can't think of a thing to apologize for, cannot see what God would need to save him from. So, since he doesn't need mercy, he doesn't need the God of mercy. Simon is unconscious of evil, and so is unsaved, unloved, unloving, lost.

Sin makes two faces. Sometimes sin is something you do—Mary did that. But sin can keep you from doing something—Simon's brand. Mary's heart was rank with weeds. But Simon's was stone cold. Jesus introduced Simon to himself that night, remorselessly, by comparing the way he had not acted to the way Mary did. Mary was moved to do something. Simon's heart and hands stood still. It was getting late so Jesus spoke roughly to raise him from the dead. "Seest thou this woman? I entered into *thy* house, *thou* gavest me no water for my feet: But *she* hath wetted my feet with her tears, and wiped them with her hair. *Thou* gavest me no kiss: But *she* since the time I came in, hath not ceased to kiss my feet. My head with oil *thou* didst not anoint: But *she* hath anointed my feet with anointment. Wherefore I say unto thee, Her sins, which are many, are forgiven; for *she* loved much: but to whom little is forgiven, the same loveth little."

The second parable was said in answer to another Simon. "Lord, how oft shall my brother sin against me, and I forgive him?" Jesus saith unto him: "I say not unto thee seven times, but until seventy times seven." Simon said seven times to be big about it, since the law only asked for three. But Jesus said seventy times seven, not to make it complicated, but to carry it out to infinity—to make sure Simon saw that mercy doesn't keep track, and the maximum mercy of which man is capable is microscopic compared to the mercy God has given us.

The parable introduces us to a man in a high position of responsibility near the king. After an auditing it was discovered he had taken 10,000 talents from the king's treasury—a simply tremendous sum. "The total annual taxes of Judea, Idumea, Samaria, Galilee, and Perea," all together "amounted to only 800 talents." The king's minister had embezzled about two million dollars and that would have created a terrible scandal even in an Oriental court. The king, naturally alarmed at such flagrant dishonesty in his own high court, "commanded him to be sold, and his wife, and children, and all that he had, and payment to be made. The servant therefore fell down, and worshipped him, saying, 'Lord, have patience with me, and I will pay thee all.' And the lord of that servant, being moved with compassion, released him, and forgave him the debt." That was more than the man could have hoped for. It was a king's pardon.

Look closely, for that man looks familiar. This is not an allegory, but the situation is a perfect likeness of ours—human, full of faults; we are in precisely the same predicament as this minister, fallen, every Adam's son of us, into a sea of the same mistakes. We have sinned in number as the sands, and are "no longer worthy to be called thy son." But God our King has pardoned us. No man has ever met himself in the light of Christ until he has associated this picture with himself. It took a cross to bring us back to life. The better the man, the better he can see what is wrong with him. The first sign of the saint is this highly developed sense of sin. The Pharisee is proud he is not like other men. The saint hangs his head that he is not like Christ. "Nowhere," said St. Francis, "is there a greater, more miserable, poorer sinner than I am."

After the shining scene of the king's mercy the picture changes and the stage is plunged into darkness. The forgiven minister is seen meeting with his servant who owes him a little money. Compared to what the minister owes the king it amounts to nothing. The minister orders the poor fellow to pay up immediately. And when the servant can't pay, the king's minister jumps up and grabs him by the throat: "'Pay me what you owe.' The man fell at his fellow-servant's feet, and begged him, 'Be patient with me, and I will pay you'; but he refused, and had him jailed until he should pay the debt."

When the minister's colleagues saw what he had done they took it to the king. And when the king heard it he was enraged and ordered the minister back into his presence, storming: "I forgave thee all that debt because thou besoughtest me, shouldst thou not also have had mercy on thy fellow servant, even as I had mercy on thee?" And the king made him take his own medicine and sent him to prison. Then Jesus said these terrifying words: "So also my heavenly Father will do to every one of you, if you do not forgive your brother from your heart."

God is not vindictive—He is not that kind. This is the parable's way of shouting that forgiveness is a matter of life and death. God gives and forgives like that. Forgiveness won't work unless it flows both ways. A man who can't give mercy, can't understand how to get it. God's forgiveness cannot flood in upon the imprisoned soul until the doors are open out of mercy from within. And the sentence we shall receive when we stand trial after death will be the verdict we gave our brother back in the jury box of life.

Kenyon J. Scudder, one of the great prison wardens of the West, liked to tell about the time a friend of his was on a train and noticed that the young man sitting next to him was feeling very low. What happened was unforgettable. The young fellow confessed that he was a convict just released from a distant penitentiary. His whole life had cast such a dark shadow over his family and they had seemed to suffer such shame from his criminal record, that he had lost almost all contact with them. He couldn't help hoping against hope however that they had forgiven him and that the almost dead silence of many years meant that they were too poor or perhaps too ill or illiterate to write. So before his prison sentence was up he had devised this plan to find out how they felt—one that would not be too hard on them or him. He wrote a letter home explaining that he would be on this train which passed their little farm at the outskirts of town. If they could forgive him they were to hang a white ribbon on the old apple tree near the tracks. If it was not hanging there when he came by he would not bother them ever again. As the train approached the familiar landmarks of his boyhood days the suspense became more than he could bear and he changed seats with his companion, who watched out the window for him. In a minute the tree was in sight and eyes bright with sudden tears his companion placed his hand on his knee and whispered hoarsely, "It's all right. The whole tree is white with ribbons."

That apple tree was speaking for heaven to that family, too, for "it is in pardoning that we are pardoned." We are all in "death row" until we decorate our trees like that. "If ye forgive men their trespasses your heavenly Father will forgive you."

> And earthly power doth then show likest God's,
> When mercy seasons justice. Therefore, Jew,
> Though justice be thy plea, consider this,
> That in the course of justice, none of us
> Should see salvation: we do pray for mercy;
> And that same prayer doth teach us all to render
> The deeds of mercy.

II

This Is His Kingdom

AND he said, "The kingdom of God is as if a man should scatter seed upon the ground, and should sleep and rise night and day, and the seed should sprout and grow, he knows not how. The earth produces of itself, first the blade, then the ear, then the full grain in the ear. But when the grain is ripe, at once he puts in the sickle, because the harvest has come."

MARK 4:26-29, Revised Standard Version

✠

HE said therefore, "What is the kingdom of God like? And to what shall I compare it? It is like a grain of mustard seed which a man took and sowed in his garden; and it grew and became a tree, and the birds of the air made nests in its branches."

And again he said, "To what shall I compare the kingdom of God? It is like leaven which a woman took and hid in three measures of meal, till it was all leavened."

LUKE 13:18-21 (also MATTHEW 13:31-33).

Revised Standard Version

6

Plant Life
        A Mustard Seed
Leaven

"MY KINGDOM," SAID Christ, "is not of this world." And men were staggered by what He said it was like. The kingdom was His favorite subject; it is our hardest—not difficult, but extremely different. Men never guessed their Messiah would be dressed like this. The world has never recovered from the shock of God's surprise attack in the stable that Christmas. The way divinity acted in the days of His flesh is as embarrassing to our sense of what is proper and practical as it was to the Pharisees. Some boys at school are busy trying to prove God didn't do the Bible, but the rest do their best to prove man didn't. It has for most of us, for all it's familiarity, a foreign, if not foolish air about it. We are as sorry as the rich young ruler, but just as sure it won't work.

But this is not man's world, He began. It is, and is to be, a Kingdom. Men, He suggested, do not make history. They have made mistakes—just look around! And they have climbed mountains—remember Moses? See Schweitzer? But the planet is, despite the devil's interference and man's two-cents'-worth, God's home-made garden. He cleared the place in space, manned it, sunned and rained it. He even made most of New York by furnishing the materials, men, and the inspiration. Man has had the opportunity to be a hero and a genius, but the Star in Christ's eyes is God. He furnished the muscle, the brains, and the good ideas. While man sleeps, "The ground produces a crop by itself."

It is very hard for man to grasp this, and that when it's all over here, and the story of earth is written up and handed in, it will not be with a "Hurrah boys" shout for the central committee, but the more moving scene of a great host of kneeling witnesses repeating together, "For Thine is the Kingdom, and the power, and the glory, forever."

The Kingdom is God's but there has been, He points out, a fiendish invasion. We cannot understand what has happened to the planet, and Christ never attempted to explain. We know only that the earth has become a great battleground and the Almighty Himself is engaged in a death struggle to get it back. Back at the beginning of our memories, men saw good and evil locked in mortal combat in the breast as on the field. Now all mankind has been swept into the conflict and it rages furiously at the edge of the abyss. The great globe itself has shrunk into a spinning cinder of its former self for fear of falling on its own sword. There can be no doubt now in anyone's mind but that the outcome of battle—hot or cold—will be close. And until the smoke of this struggle of twisted dialectics and stretched economics, which rages far out in space and deep under the sea, lifts, we cannot tell just what our chances are. But we feel we are fighting deep in our own territory now and know our backs have never been so near the wall before—jammed up almost against the goal posts of hell. We have never been less sure whether liberty and happiness shall not perish from the earth.

And in the emergency everyone is screeching at once—at the U.N., in the press, in the political parties and at tea parties.

Let us listen here to a word from the past, wrapped in a parable, from Someone who appeared at a low point in men's despair—when they used jars for tears. People had gone beyond panic and reached the hopeless state of despondency. But Someone spoke with authority and at His command faith came back again. Something this Man said or perhaps it was the way He said it, picked defeated men up off the ground and breathed the hope back into them that God could still win. By the air of sweetness and strength He had as He carried His cross right

56

into the jaws of death, and by the glory that fell on His shoulders when He emerged victorious, men have been convinced that there was something there that Lucifer and all his mutinous legions could never match. Let us take heart from Him and His parable in the darkness now. The garden was God's work. Nothing can kill it. The earth produces in spite of anything man can do. His Kingdom will come "and the gates of hell shall not prevail against it."

What does His Kingdom look like? A spot of mustard shooting up into a tree. The Kingdom is God's, it is for sure, and it starts seed-small. What an unimpressive opening day God put on for His planet: A few measly lichens on the rocks. And when the time had come for Him to come in person, He turned down Caesar and turned Himself into a child—not in a Roman Palace, but in a barn at Bethlehem. Christ Himself entered homeless and untrumpeted. The Almighty hid His Crown Jewel in a fork of hay. And when this Prince presented the top secrets of the Universe, it was not in impressively marked documents proudly locked with the Imperial Seal, but in simple parables any child could open. They are not garbled nor technical. There is no big talk about record sales or massive retaliation, no compound subjects. There is no pretension nor affected erudition. He disliked the colossal and spoke of a cup of cold water, a widow's mite, a lost boy, a man who needed help.

Men have had to mass huge armies, move mountains of groceries, immobilize nations to monopolize thrones and make an empire. God sets His up with a pocketful of seeds—a speck of love, a pinch of faith. He fed His multitude with a few loaves and two fishes, built His cross from an acorn. "The kingdom," He said, "is like a mustard seed."

It is also like leaven. It is little and it doesn't make any noise. Elijah couldn't find God in the earthquake or the storm, but in "the still small voice." The church, when it behaves, does not move "like a mighty army," but like light. God works quietly. The headachy din loyal supporters develop for their candidate at the political conventions is not the way Almighty God announced His Favorite Son: He did it with a Star. There was no clatter of hoofs, or cleats; the King of kings was born in secrecy and slipped up on mankind unnoticed in unprepossessing sandals. When men would come into His presence there would be no twenty-one-gun salute; let them kneel in silence. "Be still and know that I am God."

We will not hear His guns at Armageddon; He will take us without firing a shot. For as Sir John Seely said in speaking of the building of the new Jerusalem: "No man heard the clink of trowel or pickaxe; it descended [silently] out of heaven from God." "The kingdom of heaven is like leaven."

". . . which a woman took and hid in three measures of meal." She did not store the yeast in a box; she mixed it into the dough. Christ did not imprison the precious bird in a monastic bosom, but released it to men. But it was done under cover— the woman hid it. God will not take over His Province in Public Royal Fiat nor baptize with a heavy hand. He will not take any political nor military action at all. His love will assume command by infiltration. "Not by might, nor by power, but by my spirit, saith the Lord. . . ." Faith is not administrative but atmospheric, not learned, but breathed. Some contagious force was introduced in Christ which has spread by contact. "Andrew found Peter and Philip found Nathaniel." Stephen's dying ignited the cold hard life of Saul into the bright flame that lit the church across the first great sea. And so on from man to man the torch has been passed down in one grand Apostolic Succession.

"Until it was all leavened." We see now that "The light shines in the darkness, and the darkness has not overcome it." And beside the graves of our beloved we take heart from His will that not "one of these little ones shall perish." In the embittered rock bottom valley through which our grim day is trying to pick its way, where we can hear the shrieks of despair all about us in the darkness, we put our trust once more in Him who is fighting for the life of Everyman. He will never give us up, nor rest until the "last enemy" is destroyed, but intends to walk invisibly beside us until our hearts, too, burn within us along the way, until this old earth is at last permeated with the warmth of His radiance and all its flickering lamps at last aglow with the incandescent splendor of His Son. "The kingdom of heaven is like leaven which a woman took and hid in three measures of meal, till it was all leavened."

A GAIN, the kingdom of heaven is like unto treasure hid in a field; the which when a man hath found, he hideth, and for joy thereof goeth and selleth all that he hath, and buyeth that field. Again, the kingdom of heaven is like unto a merchant man, seeking goodly pearls: Who, when he had found one pearl of great price, went and sold all that he had, and bought it. Again, the kingdom of heaven is like unto a net, that was cast into the sea, and gathered of every kind: Which, when it was full, they drew to shore, and sat down, and gathered the good into vessels, but cast the bad away. So shall it be at the end of the world; the angels shall come forth, and sever the wicked from among the just, And shall cast them into the furnace of fire: there shall be wailing and gnashing of teeth.

MATTHEW 13:44-50, King James Version

7

The Buried Treasure
The Pearl of Great Price
The Net

THE NEAR EAST appears to be wasted space, but below that little sand lot lies an ocean of oil. The Dead Sea is the nearest place to geographical hell we can get on this planet's surface, but that godforsaken hole was where heaven kissed earth. The Book seems such an unappetizing oyster, but it cradles the Pearl. So the church, too, has something more to do than make boring assignments; drab preachers may be dying to talk dismally about tithing, but their Master died to give men gold. "The kingdom of heaven" is not man's, but God's Good Deed. It is not like an Every Member Canvass. "The kingdom of Heaven is like treasure lying buried in a field."

What treasure? First, some medicine to bring down the burning fever for speed and gadgets. Look here: This is the only operation that can successfully remove that huge goiter of guilt that makes every man sick and tired of himself, the anesthetic for the nagging ache for more. We need inspiration to replace the exhausting compulsions that penalize our age. Dig deeper in this unbelievable chest. There is an expensive perfume to refresh us from the smothering odor of prejudice. This is a mine of vital statistics, an education for underprivileged provincials who know nothing but earth. Here is a scholarship to free men from ignorance with a free peek beyond the walls of mortality. Our town is not the only place, the best way to live —there is "a still more excellent way" than piracy, a better country than Treasure Island. What's this? Man's missing blue-print—the lost directions more accurate than Captain Flint's for finding his position and his harbor. What next? A lamp to use at night, an introduction to Someone to go to in trouble, to talk to when afraid, to break the curse of loneliness.

Could this be the overlooked fountain of youth? A man's eyes cannot grow dim on its bright hope; its faith keeps him fresh. Here is a little something to "cast out all fear." No drug, but daylight. We do not have to go to the end of the rainbow. Remember the game we used to play? Cold or hot was clue to how far away. We are warmer now than De Leon. This common-looking Christian coffer holds heaven's bread and water. To taste is life and one drink is enough to last. Above all, this faith has kept untarnished the one invaluable secret men have been dying to know since they first shipwrecked upon this solar isle. His question from the beginning has been: "Do I matter to God?" One Sunday during church a little child scratched down these uneven letters uphill on a scrap of paper and handed it to her mother: "Dear Mother and Father, I love you. Do you love me? If you do love me draw an 'O' around yes or no." That, if we are man enough to admit it, is the burning adult question. And men have beat the ground with their fists and shrieked this at the sky ever since they first became conscious—"O Whoever you are, do you care or not?" This is man's perennial cry to his Maker, not only with his first scrawl but with his last breath. The right to call this Word "good news" rests here; for it insists that with His own hand He has circled "Yes." Is it not then a treasure?

Then where is it? It is both a surprise and a search. The man in our first parable stumbled onto it in a field, accidentally. Perhaps a farmer heard his plow scrape metal. And this is the way it comes to some and in some way to all—a Christmas Present. St. Paul said so—and showed it on the way to Damascus. But the second story insists you must look for it, "like a merchant seeking goodly pearls," who at last found "the pearl of great price." So our belief brings both sudden joy and lifelong pilgrimage. The Book is good news now and a beckoning note in the bottle.

There are then two ways of finding the treasure—something found for us and something we find for ourselves. But the stories agree, when found there is but one entrance, one key. Finder's Keepers only if he abandon everything else. The man who fell upon it in a field sold everything he had to buy that field. The merchant sacrificed his entire collection to secure that single pearl.

Churches put the cart before the horse, and solicit something from men who may not have found anything and unnecessarily canvass those who have found everything. The discoverers of grace give spontaneously, unsparingly. The meaning is not that men will throw their money away on the first beggar they meet. Giving up everything to buy this treasure does not require giving away all our goods to charity but to God. We are not chained to the *church's* request, but committed to "the church's one *Foundation*." Quite possibly the church is not asking a fraction of what our thankfulness is impelling us to give. The giving by the enlightened will be restrained only by their means and timing. Christian stewardship does not demand that we abdicate proprietorship of property. It asks only that we relinquish ownership and control to our Master.

But no sacrifice seems sacrifice to someone who has seen what Divinity has saved up for us. The Find is so infinite as to embarrass the most that any man can do. Both finders in this story leaped to deliver every nickel as minimum down payment. It was nothing to the incredible "everything." In contrast to the usual grave deliberations of the contemporary church pledging system, they couldn't wait, and they couldn't do enough. The very idea of overpaying God! They reacted suddenly, ecstatically. What was their two-cents'-worth when compared with "the eternal weight of glory" that was descending upon them. It was "for the joy that was set before him," that Christ paid the cross, careless of the humiliation.

The last bead He strung on this little trio of parables was the one about the dragnet. After the two stories of adventure comes one of judgment. When fishermen haul in their net they sort the catch and fling away the culls. Something like this, Jesus said, goes on in heaven. Today men blur the sharp distinctions the Bible makes between good and evil. Now heaven and hell have become very vague and hazy in our minds and by back-slapping we cheerily absolve sin and have all but joked away the very idea of hell. Badness is just a sickness and criminals are merely psychotic. Men may make themselves believe this. Not the wildest imagination could make God say it. Earth's not the pet shop of an indulgent breeder. He used a mirror to mold us and He expects us to act like Him too. We are not going to give up God's mercy here, but anyone can see in this story a streak of justice. His creation has some standards, and we must stand inspection. There is discipline along with and in order to have kindness. We are not safe in some fire-proof nursery sieved of pins. In the midst of Eden there grows a tree. "Thou shalt not eat of it: for in the day that thou eatest thereof thou shalt surely die." This world has its promise of buried treasure —but peril too—its Truth or Consequences.

Many have difficulty believing in an angry God blaming men for their fathers' guilt, and retaliating unmercifully forever for their few years of mortal crime. But we may not be so bright as we believe. Before we go on looking with such condescension on our Puritan forebears we had best confess we may have swung so far as to strike the reefs on the other side of the channel. Taking hell out of creation takes away the terrible urgency, the major importance, with which the Bible invests it. If we take away the penalties the game of life is soon a purposeless farce and victory unclear and uninviting. Out goes joy and exultation with the rules. If life is not a matter of life and death then our decisions make less and less difference and the quality that Christ packed into existence leaks away. We may take away the gospel's bitter "fire and brimstone" taste but perhaps it's time, too, to stop mixing it so sickeningly sweet.

This selection ends, suspicious that these three parables shall exist long after our own fragile viewpoint has been extinct. And they at least are sure that God has lovingly given us the treasure and also, in "fear and trembling," the choice.

AND they said to him, "The disciples of John fast often and offer prayers, and so do the disciples of the Pharisees, but yours eat and drink." And Jesus said to them, "Can you make wedding guests fast while the bridegroom is with them? The days will come, when the bridegroom is taken away from them, and then they will fast in those days." He told them a parable also: "No one tears a piece from a new garment and puts it upon an old garment; if he does, he will tear the new, and the piece from the new will not match the old. And no one puts new wine into old wineskins; if he does, the new wine will burst the skins and it will be spilled, and the skins will be destroyed. But new wine must be put into fresh wineskins. And no one after drinking old wine desires new; for he says, 'The old is good.'"

LUKE 5:33-39 (also MATTHEW 9:14-17, MARK 2:18-22),
Revised Standard Version

✠

"HAVE you understood all this?" They said to him, "Yes." And he said to them, "Therefore every scribe who has been trained for the kingdom of heaven is like a householder who brings out of his treasure what is new and what is old."

MATTHEW 13:51, 52, Revised Standard Version

8

The Bridal Party
   The Patch
New Wine in an Old Wineskin
   A Man Who Had Something Old and
   Something New

"WHY DON'T YOUR disciples fast?" The question did not come
out of idle curiosity but red-hot contradiction. The conservatives
really wanted to know: "Why don't you do things the way they
have always been done?" Jesus gave convention an appalling
jolt. When He said: "Ye have heard that it hath been said by
them of old time. . . . But I say unto you," custom was horrified
and complained bitterly, like badly shaken money-changers from
behind upturned tables: "Who said you could?" Palestine simply
could not understand why Jesus could not behave and be a good
Jew. Tradition never likes to be disturbed and no one needs to
read very far in the New Testament to find He was too big
for the Pharisees' tight religious system. The only fast that
Moses demanded was Yom Kippur on the Day of Atonement,
but through the years fasts multiplied like flies until a man
could be proud to pray in public: "I fast twice in the week."
Jesus paid His life to break it up. The Jews joined the Romans
to crush Christianity for having "turned the world upside
down."

But the thing that made all the difference in the world in

His religion was pure joy. Religion had become a carefully preserved antique—no one must laugh out loud or jump up and down for fear of falling on it. Religion had come to mean monastic caution, retreat, a mad competition in restraint among the professionals. Jesus made it break into smiles. He did not make fun of it, but fun out of it. Religion threw the book of restrictions at the Pharisees; it put the fear of God into John the Baptist's men; it made Jesus very happy. Men took their faith like a funeral with frowns and fasts; He took it like a wedding, feasting. There would still be time for tears, but God is not our Taskmaster, but our Father. Earth is not His footstool, but His bride; death is not doom, but glory. He was overjoyed at the birth of Christianity and passed out this gay parable to stump the grumpy experts: "Can you make wedding guests fast while the bridegroom is with them?"

But the next parable shows Jesus protecting the precious faith of His fathers from His fresh ideas. It may have come to Him while watching Mary mending. "And no one puts a piece of unshrunk cloth on an old garment, for the patch tears away from the garment, and a worse tear is made." He did not want to keep His highly inflammable belief in the same old doctrinal building for fear of setting fire to it. The temple was too old and delicate to hold such a new burst of faith. Christianity must have a new coat to wear or split its father's down the back. If He put His words in with the Talmud they would tear it to shreds. The Old Covenant was not compatible with the New and must be separated for the old one's sake.

But that parable, and its twin especially, is concerned for the safety of Christianity. "And no one puts new wine into old wineskins; if he does, the new wine will burst the skins and it will be spilled." The Good News must not sail in the context of Judaism or it will go down with the ship. The waves of legislation in the Talmud would clog, cause friction, confusion. But frankly, the Old Agreement had had its day—otherwise He would have no excuse for contradicting it with "a New Covenant." Judaism crystallized long ago and was simply too inflexible to adapt, too crowded to make room, for such a creative child as the Gospel. Frail B.C. could never cradle virile A.D.

This parable can be taken personally. No one's conversion will keep in the same old mental surroundings. If a man is to be better, he must move to a better moral environment—else all his resolutions will eventually take their former seats. We cannot take this breath of fresh air back into the same stuffy place where we used to live without losing it. We are not speaking geographically, but insisting that old associations can disease a fledgling faith. A recently cleaned heart can easily pick up grime from off the walls of the way we used to be, soon diluting the new quality beyond recognition. New vows must have a new leaf of study habits, reading lists, new faces to fit the new criterion. Life must have more windows, a better view, more room to handle the height and sight of the new spirit. "No man puts new wine into old wineskins."

Besides, the Gospel is not merely an amendment to the Old Testament, but a brand new motion of faith, a dream come true—according to orthodoxy, too good to be true—not an appendix patched on, but another book. A bigger and better synagogue would not do. This new congregation of ideas demanded that ground be broken for a Cathedral. The new wine needed a new place to go.

After all, the important thing is not the bottle, but the wine. Men spend too much time admiring the wineskin. Naturally we want to find a satisfactory form of worship, but that is only the container and must not be confused with the contents. Men freeze to styles that should have been stored in attics long ago. They honor shrines instead of the spirit of God that may have moved since then, they confuse creeds with the real thing the creed is about, and love the lovely letters of King James instead of Him whom no language nor achitecture can own. The old skins make lovely museum pieces, but we do not worship dead wood, cold stone, but the living God who cannot be chained to any prison of words nor ways of doing things. Christianity must have a place to stay, but it does not have to stay there. It is eternally young and will outwear any translation of it, any church built for it. This parable predicts it will make itself at home in any solar system in stratospheric space as it has in Gothic, Colonial or Quaker Meeting House. It is a jewel in any setting. Tragically, almost all the denominational quarreling has been over which pail to use to carry the belief, but God can use ravens and say things several ways at once. No man must lose his faith just because some old bottle of dogmatism burst. We must not run the risk of spilling truth by idolatrous hanging on too long to some old oaken bucket. "New wine must be put into fresh wineskins."

But it would not be fair to call Jesus a revolutionist and stop there. "I came not to destroy but to fulfil." Luke adds this conservative line to the parable of the wineskins: "And no man having drunk old wine desireth new." The last parable takes up this point. "The kingdom of heaven is like unto a man . . . who bringeth forth out of his treasure things new *and* old." Communists hate history; Jesus never did such a thing. Jesus used soap on the past, not acid; water, not fire. His debt to the past was gigantic. He took most of the New Testament from the Old. He was steeped in its psalms and His speech was saturated with the prophecies. The greatest commandment of all He found in two pieces way back in the Book where it had been all the time.

Truth goes through one suit after another, but it is still the truth. Christian fashions come and go but "Jesus Christ the same yesterday, and to day, and for ever." Jesus did not follow in His Father's footsteps, but beyond in the same direction. He did not reject the past, but started from there. He traveled into a new world, but it was the same journey Abraham began.

Nothing is wrong with the new just because it's new. The old deserves our respect—it could not have lived so long without merit. It was new—once. But our faith does not sanctify the Christian furniture of any period; it lives in them all, loves the best of each. Old patterns are not "millstones," but as Buttrick believes, "milestones." Christianity can feel secure doing other things than looking up its ancestry. It likes other languages just as well as Latin and is able to believe that God has spoken and men have heard since the seventeenth century. Christianity does not collect fossils, but things that will work. It is not a museum but a live operation. And "Eye hath not seen nor ear heard, neither have entered into the heart of man, the things which God hath prepared. . . ." We cannot be too conservative else we shall never be able to leave earth and face heaven. After all, Jesus was regarded as an extreme liberal in His day and He was killed by the rank conservatives. It was the liberals in 1776 who led the American Revolution and the conservative Tories who turned back to England.

Men still divide into two camps, one applying the brakes, the other accelerating; one group caressing antiques, the other in love with the latest models. Christianity does not vote a straight ticket—it selects treasures from both old and new. It believes our father's God is our God today with more to say. It respects the past and the future, so the future may one day be a past to deserve respect. It will not have the old and the new at swords points, but in perfect combination. Faith takes old men, young men, tradition in addition to adventure. It will not be reckless nor hidebound, but it will go to the ends of the earth, to the end of time, in whatever transportation is available.

So Christ made Moses over new. The same words long familiar in precious scrolls were now newly bound in Him. The everlasting face of God the Father became visible in the expression of His new Son. God is not interested in the Age. He may even make "a new heaven and a new earth," but He will stay right where He is. We take some of both, judging by the light, not time, for "The kingdom of heaven is like unto a man . . . who bringeth forth out of his treasure things new and old."

*H**E put another parable before them. "The Realm of heaven," he said, "is like a man who sowed good seed in his field, but while men slept his enemy came and resowed weeds among the wheat and then went away. When the blade sprouted and formed the kernel, then the weeds appeared as well. So the servants of the owner went to him and said, 'Did you not sow good seed in your field, sir? How then does it contain weeds?' He said to them, 'An enemy has done this.' The servants said to him, 'Then would you like us to go and gather them?' 'No,' he said, 'for you might root up the wheat when you were gathering the weeds. Let them both grow side by side till harvest; and at harvest-time I will tell the reapers to gather the weeds first and tie them in bundles to be burnt, but to collect the wheat in my granary.'"*

MATTHEW 13:24-30, James Moffatt

✠

THEN he left the crowds and went indoors. His disciples came up to him saying, "Explain to us the parable of the weeds in the field." So he replied, "He who sows the good seed is the Son of man; the field is the world; the good seed means the sons of the Realm; the weeds are the sons of the evil one; the enemy who sowed them is the devil; the harvest is the end of the world, and the reapers are the angels. Well then, just as the weeds are gathered and burnt in the fire, so shall it be at the end of the world; the Son of man will despatch his angels, and they will gather out of his Realm all who are hindrances and who practise iniquity, throwing them into the furnace of fire; there men will wail and gnash their teeth. Then shall the just shine like the sun in the Realm of their Father. He who has an ear, let him listen to this."

MATTHEW 13:36-43, James Moffatt

9

The Tares

"ANOTHER PARABLE HE set before them, saying, The kingdom of heaven is likened unto a man that sowed good seed in his field: but while men slept, his enemy came and sowed tares also among the wheat, and went away."

Earth's population is polluted with the "bad guys"—they grow like bad weeds on both sides of the tracks, on both sides of the question, the ocean, the college degree. Even God's own flock is filled with black sheep. The pews of first church are not neat rows in a clean garden, but rank with the misplaced. What happened? It is an unbearable and embarrassing riddle. How did the snake ever get into God's Garden in the beginning? Theologians are still grinding out endless shelves of heavy speculation. Jesus put His explanation in this simply fascinating "whodunit?"

Evil is not in the imagination. His story admits that evil exists and is here to stay until that day. Someone has "sowed tares among the wheat" and this has choked some of the crop and created a crisis for the rest. It is a depressing thought, but an impressive one too. As bad as it is to have evil surrounding us, how much better to be aware of it. Man's consciousness of evil is one of the wonders of the world. It takes something wonderful in us to see that something is wrong. How much worse life would be if we did not know enough, feel enough, to wonder and to wish. Hell is jammed with men who don't know any better than to be happy there. We are not ashamed to ask and Jesus was not afraid to answer, "Where has the darnel come from?"

It is the perfect crime, and Christ, of course, did not completely solve it—that was not necessary. It might satisfy our curiosity but it would not assist our salvation. We spend too much time looking for someone to blame instead of taking some. But Jesus did perform a spectacular service. He completely cleared the skirts of

God. Not only is God not guilty—"An enemy has done this." It would be hard to measure our debt to Him for establishing God's innocence, for He has been suspect since the crime was first reported. Evil has embarrassed every religion, but Christianity has never for a moment questioned the honest face of God, that "in him," at least, "is no darkness at all." God's Son did descend into hell, but the Creed makes clear that the Maker of heaven and earth never made hell. Only "Every good gift and every perfect gift is from above." God "sowed good seed in his field . . . And while men slept, an enemy came and sowed tares also."

"While men slept"—is that the clue? That is enough evidence to convict us as accomplice if not ringleader. We are implicated not because we have been rash, but sedentary. This story unearths fresh evidence. Evil is something spawned while kindness naps. A good garden demands constant attention. Evil vines creep in to choke while loving care is in a coma. This parable points out that part of sin's secret is sleeping men.

But the next question pops up quickly. "Why doesn't gardener God get rid of the weeds?" These troublemakers threaten the crop and torture the wheat. Why risk the harvest and prolong the agony? God has a good reason for waiting: "Then do you want us to go and gather them? But he said, No; lest in gathering the weeds you root up the wheat along with them."

God holds back His hoe first for fear of making a mistake. He wants time to tell which are His and which belong below. He knows, but He waits for our fruits to identify us. This is not to say that no Christian can ever be sure that he is a "son of light," but it is to say that his certainty is in the realm of faith, not in special advance information. This parable is a corrective to those who are noisily and superficially usurping God's judicial responsibility. There is a danger in overconfidence for it leads to complacency and arrogance. What we are sure of is not ourselves, but God. And some who assume they are sincere in belief may be surprised to find that they have been fooling themselves. When someone pried: "Lord, are there few that be saved?" Jesus as much as told the man to mind his business here: "Strive to enter in at the strait gate." No one preached predestination harder than Jonathan Edwards, but according to his diary there were many days when he had misgivings about his own election. Who can be sure just what good or evil is germinating in him? The darnel that Jesus was thinking of looks just like wheat—until threshing time. But if regeneration is supposed to show up in deeds, who has done anything that looks even faintly like the second-mile deeds of love that identified the disciples? An honest look is enough to make a man pray for more time and mercy. Others, like wheat, do not always show their true colors until the last. A life may send out unforeseen shoots—like the thief on the cross. Who knows how many Pasternaks Russia may produce, or if among the hot-bed of Communists there are Tolstoys in the bud? "Let both grow together until the harvest." Then it will be safer and more appropriate to announce just which is wheat and which is "Like chaff which the wind driveth away."

But God reserves judgment for a better reason. If weeds were all pulled up now good plants would be uprooted with them. Good and evil are so entangled in this world that to extract the bad tooth may take its neighbor's life. The late Joseph Welch was conscious of the inevitable guilt that tarnishes the people as they carry out capital punishment. The electric chair is a murder weapon too. Cleaning up the church rolls may damage the active list. Rooting out a troublemaker may injure the peace of the church more than his presence. Every time a son is excommunicated, a mother is badly hurt. The inquisition doubtless got rid of some bad wood, but it also ripped out walnut in the process. Courageous saints went down in the flames of the burning stakes, and the faithful men who lit the fires for heretics became fanatical, and badly burned themselves with the hatred and hardness always required of the executioners. Poisoning rats can be suicidal. The present crisis offers a dramatic illustration. A Hiroshima slaughters little babies by the thousands. We have come to the place where we are almost afraid to shoot for fear of killing our own men. Our megatonic cartridges are almost as dangerous to those who fire them as to the target. There is not an honest man among us who would not die for the God and the freedom our fathers gave us—both far more precious to us than life itself. Patrick Henry's ringing words still cling to our lips: "Give me liberty or give me death!" But the pressure under which we're living now forces us to think over again what the Almighty meant when He said: "Vengeance is mine." And this parable ought to make us look up for a moment from checking our ammunition and listen. "Let both grow together until the harvest." "Lest in gathering the weeds you root up the wheat along with them."

But the issue of good and evil will not be left forever undecided. One day He will settle up once and for all. God delays, but He has not deserted the bench. "And at harvest time I will tell the reapers, Gather the weeds first and bind them in bundles to be burned, but gather the wheat into my barn."

The whole parable points to Providence. God, invisible and anonymous though He is, has charge of Operation Earth. The weeds have not taken over; His hand is stayed because it is sure and steady and scrupulous—to give us every chance to grow, that even the short time left may be turned to golden grain. The stamping of dictators' cleats, the thumping of Communist fists, or even the pounding we take from evil everywhere, does not come from Headquarters nor signify His resignation. The Universe is still under His command and in His own good time He will sweep up the mess and salvage the good. The days of every barren tree are numbered. Evil cannot last in the place where God makes a Garden. "For thine is the kingdom, and the power, and the glory. . . ."

This brings us now to the perplexing question of damnation. If the presence of evil presents a problem, its removal makes the problem of its presence seem elemental. How can a loving Father sentence one of His little ones—no matter how mean he may become—without being a monster? After all, is He really Sovereign if He cannot at last draw all men unto Himself? Is it fair for Him to fool around with a Creation which yields only one or two righteous per million of seed planeted? How can the Good Shepherd ever enjoy heaven so long as there is one sheep left outside?

But while we hope, and have grounds for it, that hell is corrective, not condemnatory, the Testament never encourages us to count on it. This parable leaves us with the feeling that God never forces His way into the human will, but leaves it free to choose heaven or hell for itself. And we wonder if men had life all to do over again, would they do it differently from the first time? And would those who sniped against God here, or snubbed Him, freely enjoy Him forever?

Whatever possibilities exist on that unknown side of reality, and we cannot help but trust that the tragedies here may have a happy ending there, the Bible speaks of earth's outcome with an air of awful finality. The Good News is given to us with a note of terrible urgency, as if God is not playing with us as a cat a mouse. It declares this life to be in a state of emergency. This is not one of many offers of divine hospitality—this is the only one we know about. Our acceptance of the invitation mailed to earth is for keeps. "Once to every man and nation comes the moment to decide." Birth means our time has come. How ridiculous to speculate a golden opportunity will come again. This is the growing season and one day comes the harvest.

It is not a threat but a promise. Our age bitterly resents the very idea of the last judgment. Good God would never do such a thing to dear little us. But we know better. He expects more of us than of animals. Authorities are telling us that adolescents suffer now from the absence of authority and challenge, that adults work better under pressure. How kind it was of Him to set a deadline —to be indignant at foul play, to let no man get away with murder. Far more ominous would be the fear that nothing would ever come of the fight of good and evil, the score to remain forever in the air. It is not the certainty of justice that drives men insane but the terrible uncertainty, the shattering inconsistency, the infinity of indecision that leads to panic and despair. It is good of God to be definite.

At first thought this parable may appear to present a brutal and primitive philosophy, but when one compares it to the prevalent dogmatically materialistic philosophy that now permeates campus-and novel, which has wiped out the next world and taken God out of the picture, creating a cruel emptiness in which life is only one breath of fresh air, then finished, this parable appears quaint and kind. Compared to modern cynicism that acts on vision like a vise, which makes life forever unfair, forever unreconciled, the crooked never made straight, wrongs never righted by any more than the tinkering hand of man; compared to the casual faithlessness of much of modern times that thinks of life, when it thinks at all, as a piece of business, forever unfair, unfinished; compared to that undisciplined, wasteful view that does not care whether the angels among us, and the golden shred of goodness in us perishes or not; compared to that, how kind it was of Him to say: "and at harvest time. . . ."

WHEN one of those who sat at table with him heard this, he said to him, "Blessed is he who shall eat bread in the kingdom of God!" But he said to him, "A man once gave a great banquet, and invited many; and at the time for the banquet he sent his servant to say to those who had been invited, 'Come; for all is now ready.' But they all alike began to make excuses. The first said to him, 'I have bought a field, and I must go out and see it; I pray you, have me excused.' And another said, 'I have bought five yoke of oxen, and I go to examine them; I pray you, have me excused.' And another said, 'I have married a wife, and therefore I cannot come.' So the servant came and reported this to his master. Then the householder in anger said to his servant, 'Go out quickly to the streets and lanes of the city, and bring in the poor and maimed and blind and lame.' And the servant said, 'Sir, what you commanded has been done, and still there is room.' And the master said to the servant, 'Go out to the highways and hedges, and compel people to come in, that my house may be filled. For I tell you, none of those men who were invited shall taste my banquet.' "
LUKE 14:15-24 (also MATTHEW 22:1-10),

Revised Standard Version

✠

"BUT when the king came in to look at the guests, he saw there a man who had no wedding garment; and he said to him, 'Friend, how did you get in here without a wedding garment?' And he was speechless. Then the king said to the attendants, 'Bind him hand and foot, and cast him into the outer darkness; there men will weep and gnash their teeth.' For many are called, but few are chosen."

MATTHEW 22:11-14, Revised Standard Version

10

A Prince's Wedding Banquet
The Wedding Guest Not Dressed for a Wedding

"A MAN ONCE gave a great banquet, and invited many." According to Matthew that man was a king, and the banquet was a marriage feast for his son. The gospel truth is that God's Kingdom of Heaven is comparable to just such a perfectly marvelous time as that.

That picture has been lost as it was lost on Simon, the Pharisee, who heard the parable for the first time. The idea that any godly gathering could be fun is preposterous. There is much more of the grave than of birth in the prevalent image of the church. Even Christmas has to be made up by painting on a lipstick-red Santa Claus smile. Church, in our minds, is more funeral than wedding, and carries a heavy-hearted solemnity that outlaws laughter. One wonders what the undertaker would do with an Easter shriek of joy. Any sign of gaiety would appall the pallbearers. Members think of an outsider as one who ought to have his shoulder to the wheel—it does not occur to them to say: "Poor fellow doesn't know what he's missing." We agree everyone ought to be in church; but we don't consider it such a delightful must as to call men fools for turning it down. The Sunday school is draped with compulsion because that's the way we feel about it. Most find they can wait to keep the Sabbath day. Our idea of a good time was divorced from goodness ages ago. We aim at dignity in our services not happiness.

But this parable has the nerve to insist that God is the life of the party; that we do not know what it is to have a good time until we have celebrated with Him. The gospel stands for "good news." It skips on the wings of thrilling expectation. Every Cinderella is invited to God's Open House. But the ballrooms of fairy tales and earthly monarchs can hardly match the palace of the King of Heaven. The second birth does demand sacrifice, but that fee is drowned in supernatural splendor. "The kingdom of heaven may be compared to a king who gave a marriage feast for his son, and sent his servants to call those who were invited."

"But they would not come." Is it possible that men would toss such a royal invitation into the wastebasket? One would assume there would be a skyrocketing black-market scramble for seats. Surely anyone asked to come to that heavenly mansion would break all engagements, stand forever in endlessly long lines and pay anything to get in. But no. To the king's utter consternation, "They all alike began to make excuses."

"The first said to him, 'I have bought a field, and I must go out and see it; I pray you, have me excused.'" Now this man is no profligate, turning down the king's invitation to attend something thrown by the devil. He's a good man like almost all the villains in Jesus' parables. He is decent, law-abiding, respectable. The trouble with him is that he is too busy. On the surface his excuse is a good one, but God knows, as any host would know, that any such chronic reply is giving priority to his job and insults the host to second place. The man said he *must* see his field. The truth is he *wanted* to see his field. The tally of our decisions tattles where our heart is. This is the only excuse we have from this man. Obviously Jesus meant it to be representative. This man worships work and makes light of God.

"And another said, 'I have bought five yoke of oxen, and I go to examine them; I pray you, have me excused.'" Now there is nothing wrong with hitching up new oxen. But there is something wrong with switching them ahead of God. Double-checking an investment is a good idea, but a poor excuse for rejecting his superior's hospitality. Jesus never really preached much against the conventional concept of immorality. But He spent many of His parables discrediting very moral, very busy men, who didn't have time for excellence. His quarrel was almost never with the "bad guys" but with men who put good things before the best. Jesus spent much of His time on the first commandment, which is, as its position indicates, the basic issue of religion. God must have first place in a man's life. If He doesn't, then He is not God in the life of that man.

"And another said, 'I have married a wife, and therefore I cannot come.'" Surely a man could be excused from church for a honeymoon. A family is unquestionably sacred and ought to have a higher priority than it now enjoys, but it too is subordinate to life's main business. But if God is excluded from the most precious moments of marriage, why bring Him in for dregs? No matter how much is made of it, there is a previous question to "Can this marriage be saved?" And if it is not answered well it won't matter much if the marriage is saved. A man blandly takes a vacation from God without realizing how shrilly that declares his independence from God. He would never think of taking a vacation without his wife. If that does not say who is head of the house, it does show that God is not. A man's job, his friends, his home, were not meant to take first place. And no wise wife would ever try to take the King's seat. She is much safer sitting at His feet. Something tragic is afoot when these good things cease to serve God and start serving as excuses to be away from Him. They are not meant to sidetrack us, but to express us to Him. Life is all of a piece, and if a man is Christian, every finger in his every pie will belong to that God-armed hand.

We have all made excuses to God. Someone keeps repeating, "I got too much religion when I was a boy." That might mean he was fed the wrong kind the wrong way. More likely it is a lame apology for carrying on his mutiny. Another complains, "I must spend Sundays with my family." But what good is a godless man to anyone? No family will enjoy Sundays together very much or very long without God.

Why do men ask to be excused from heaven? Perhaps they don't know what they are missing—they do not have faith it could be fun. They fear His feast will be deadly—draped with Pharisees. Perhaps the messengers distort the invitation. Is that the reason why men try to get out of going? No. Something is wrong with man. Genesis reports man fell and hurt himself and has never been the same since. Explain it how you will, there is something that makes us say "No" to God and before we know it, we are making up cute little excuses. But this is what life is for—to give us time to make up our minds about heaven.

What happens if we refuse? In this parable the king was furious when they wouldn't come. And he roared: "None of those men who were invited shall taste my banquet." Now God is no petulant child getting back at those who hurt His feelings. The parable is suggesting that mortality is our chance, that there is something conclusive about our life here. Our death signals the end, not of an inning, but a game. All God's mercy cannot erase that final score. And while "the grave is not the goal," "life is real, life is earnest." We know that death will bring with it new horizons. Nonetheless, for all the limitations of this life it has opportunities peculiar to it for "heaven's sake" that even heaven does not have. And when we lose this life, we will lose an advantage that belonged to it alone. We know our Host is merciful. What we are respecting here is the guest's awesome privilege to refuse.

"None of those men who were invited shall taste my banquet." This is the only invitation we shall ever receive that really matters. God is offering us life. It is the only offer ever made to man. To refuse is suicide. Jesus caught these "excuse makers" in the act. Notice how true it is for as far as we can see; only God has the facilities to feast us properly. Other gods prove false. Men hitch their wagons to a star, but stars grow cold. Men love flesh, but flesh decays. Men adore their wives, but wives won't hold up divinely. Men adore their homes, but homes break up. To defy God is to ask for death.

Then what will God do if He destroys His first invitation list? After the messengers reported, "The king was furious. . . . Then he said . . . 'The wedding-feast is ready; but the guests I invited did not deserve the honour. Go out to the main thoroughfares, and invite everyone you can find.' . . . So the hall was packed with guests."

God will not let our stubbornness ruin His celebration. If we won't come, He will find men who will. If the Jews won't listen He will turn to the Gentiles, and if they won't, He will go across the tracks—the poor will hear gladly. He will leave town to try country shepherds and search far for the wise. He will let the Inn alone to visit the stable, and pass over adults to invite a child. Jesus was the most patient of men to those behind bars. The ones who exasperated Him were the morally superior citizens who couldn't spare a time for time's Maker. And this parable is one of the most devastating pronouncements against good men ever made. They are excluded from paradise by their own wish. This parable transfers to heaven those they have sent to hell. The prostitutes will get into heaven before the Pharisees will. It makes our destination an open question. Vachel Lindsay caught the ragged Salvation Army crew with which Christ was populating paradise.

> Booth led boldly with his big bass drum—
> * * *
> The Saints smiled gravely and they said, "He's come."
> * * *
> Walking lepers followed, rank on rank,
> Lurching bravos from the ditches dank,
> * * *
> Vermin-eaten saints with moldy breath,
> Unwashed legions with the ways of Death. . . .

Jesus was not exalting the sinner. He was saying that the flophouse bum would overtake the inattentive proud to St. Peter's Gate. Superficially fine moral character doesn't impress the court of heaven. The issue is: "Has a man humbled himself before God and become obedient?"

The last parable takes us into the banquet hall. Everything is ready to begin. There is a flourish of trumpets. The king enters. But as he looks over his guests his eye falls on a man without a wedding garment. The way he is dressed does not signify poverty but impudence. The man had casually drifted into the king's ball as if it did not deserve preparation. The king, eager to believe there is some good explanation for such a gross error, inquires: "Friend, how did you get in here without a wedding garment?" The man didn't bother to reply. There was rudeness in his manner as his dress. Others had made light of the kingdom by their flimsy excuses and stayed away. This man made light of it by coming. The king, hating hypocrisy most, had him tied up and thrown out.

How close this comes to all of us. Making the motions of Christianity but laughing inwardly. Publicly vowing membership, but ridiculing the meaning in private. How many of us how many times have sauntered into the Presence, puttering about with prayer with not the slightest thought of really doing anything about interior redecoration? How many of us are inwardly dressed with righteousness? "Except ye repent," said Jesus—to whom did He say this? We know: "Ye shall all likewise perish." "Turn back, O man, forswear thy foolish ways." It is time for all of us to get dressed. The King cometh.

III

This Is Your Duty

A_{ND} he spake many things unto them in parables, saying, Behold, a sower went forth to sow; And when he sowed, some seeds fell by the way side, and the fowls came and devoured them up: Some fell upon stony places, where they had not much earth: and forthwith they sprung up, because they had no deepness of earth: And when the sun was up, they were scorched; and because they had no root, they withered away. And some fell among thorns; and the thorns sprung up, and choked them: But other fell into good ground, and brought forth fruit, some an hundredfold, some sixtyfold, some thirtyfold. Who hath ears to hear, let him hear.

MATTHEW 13:3-9, King James Version

✛

H_{EAR} ye therefore the parable of the sower. When any one heareth the word of the kingdom, and understandeth it not, then cometh the wicked one, and catcheth away that which was sown in his heart. This is he which received seed by the way side. But he that received the seed into stony places, the same is he that heareth the word, and anon with joy receiveth it; Yet hath he not root in himself, but dureth for a while: for when tribulation or persecution ariseth because of the word, by and by he is offended. He also that received seed among the thorns is he that heareth the word; and the care of this world, and the deceitfulness of riches, choke the word, and he becometh unfruitful. But he that received seed into the good ground is he that heareth the word, and understandeth it; which also beareth fruit, and bringeth forth, some an hundredfold, some sixty, some thirty.
MATTHEW 13:18-23 (also MARK 4:2-8,

LUKE 8:4-8, 11-15), King James Version

11

The Sower

"A SOWER WENT forth to sow." But this is not a story about a sower nor his seed. They will not be seen again. The rest of this parable is about the soil that was sowed. This switches the light off the Book and the pulpit and shines it on the man in the pew. The hero or the villain in this story is you, and the plot is how well you pay attention.

After all, the thing that makes worship succeed is not a good sermon, but good ears. The choir may robe to be ready for the eyes-front order of service, but the chancel is not a stage. The minister is not the starring actor. Don't let the bulletins fool you. The place to watch in church is where the people are. Perhaps the sermon should be chewed well after church, but it is not gum but bread. And the ultimate objective of the sermon is not to raise provocative questions but to give life. So the hopes and fears of the Christian faith focus not on the seed, for that is sure, nor in the sower, for he's not so important, but on the uneven ground where the Good News falls.

Sometimes the sower is at fault for Christianity's crop failure. Some ministers broadcast their own ideas instead of good seed. Others drill the Word with such blasphemous dullness that it cannot be said to be sowed well. Church records are filled and church pews are emptied by the glaring defects of the clergy. But the pulpit has been filled by towering giants too—and they have failed. One of the great preachers of this century confided near the close of his life that, no matter how magnificent others thought his ministry, he could not name a single man that he had brought to Christ. That confession is a tribute to a great man's humility, but also makes pitifully clear that the minister's success is at the mercy of his audience. Some of our greatest prophets know from heartbreaking personal experience what it is to have "toiled all the night, and have taken nothing." Should they be penalized? "And he did not many mighty works" in His home town, not because He did not do His best, but "because of their unbelief." And when His breathtaking miracles happened, He did not credit His finesse, but their faith. This soil story suggests that the bottleneck lies in the back of the heads at the back of the church.

The parable promotes the listener from the lowest order of comprehension to the highest place of responsibility. This places anyone who hears the Word of God preached under the awful obligation, not to criticize or compliment, but to decide. For no ingenious method of treating the seed or scattering it can make up for the final "say so" of the soil. As Jesus said of those stubbornly stone deaf, "Neither will they be persuaded, though one rose from the dead." The sower can only go so far. The rest is up to you. "Take heed what ye hear."

"Some seeds fell by the wayside." Much of the gospel "goes in one ear and out the other"—it never germinates. The seed was good, and the preacher planted it. But it never got under the skin. "Many are called, but few are chosen." No wonder Calvin concluded so many seem elected to be damned. Just look at those who couldn't care less about being shown "a more excellent way." The Bible lies perpetually at the bottom of their reading list. St. Chrysostom could preach until he was blue in the face to our TV time, and how many listening millions would say, "That's very interesting," but would make no promises? People live through weekend after lost weekend, the next verse the same as the first, and on and on monotonously to the bitter end. It doesn't take a Calvin to make their spiritual forecast. It will read from here to eternity: "No change." Failure dogs the sower's steps. Most of his precious time is wasted! Anyone who has ever tried to tell the truth of God must be able not only to take defeat, but trampling. There are so many who think what he says is simply as the parable says, "for the birds," and it is callously kicked by careless feet.

But this is the gamble he takes. A sower can't stop planting for fear it won't grow. In St. Paul's Cathedral there is a bronze tablet to the memory of Canon Samuel A. Barnett, who preached undaunted in hard East London for half a century. On the tablet is a figure of a sower, walking down the furrows of a field. Underneath the figure the words: "Fear not to sow on account of the birds." So we do not lose heart.

"Other seeds fell on rocky ground, where they had not much soil, and immediately they sprang up, since they had no depth of soil, but when the sun rose they were scorched; and since they had no root they withered away." There are some to whom Christianity is "easy come, easy go." They are converts on the first ballot but they have no growing roots that go deep to endure to the end. Not all those that the revival reports saved, backslide. There is an embarrassing handful of men like "wee Davy Livingstone" whose height dwarfs many who have mumbled their vows on the soft chancel carpet. Some men, of course, can swear easily on the sawdust, swayed by the fever pitch excitement instead of the Holy Spirit, and begin to build something they won't be able to finish.

For below the skinny surface of human life is a bone of desire to keep things the way they are. Beneath the inviting make-up paint, hearts are paved with "hands-off" policies, policed against any invasion of the will of God. Any new commitment soon comes up against a wall of stubborn security measures that resist any good Samaritan risk. Men have become habit-hardened to a demanding traffic of elegant tastes. All they want is to live in the style to which they have become accustomed—so all they want is a little bit more. Under such sustained pressures from the ego, the subsoil of their lives has solidified. Once, years ago, these men no doubt meant to keep their confirmation vows, but at the height of success, the high noon of temptation, their superficial resolutions wilted and their shallow roots were scorched.

"Other seeds fell upon thorns, and the thorns grew up and choked them." This is the saddest part of this parable—soil that could produce greatness, but it is growing a jungle. The problem is not stones, but weeds. Sir Gawain's shallow interest in the Holy Grail soon shriveled up, but the valiant Launcelot failed in the search, not for lack of depth, but from the "squeeze play" of an unpruned vine: lust for Arthur's queen. He confessed without flinching.

> . . . But in me lived a sin
> So strange, of such a kind, that all of pure,
> Noble and knightly in me twined and clung
> Round that one sin, until the wholesome flower
> And poisonous grew together, each as each,
> Not to be plucked asunder.

This point of the parable is sharp enough to prick us all to the quick. It is unbearably good contemporary biography. In a stroke, Christ has drawn a devastating cartoon of the contemporary Christian whose fields are fertile but so riddled with competing interests they are strangling the struggling Christian shoots. Weeds need not be wicked to be weeds. They are more often good plants in the wrong place. That is what America suffers from. Our heads are buzzing with so many good ideas we don't have time for the best. Christianity is fighting a losing battle in so many of our lives, not because we are bad, but because we are too busy with our briefcaseful of second rate stuff. These Christians caught in the briar patch are men of fertile imagination, rich in depth, capable of being His Crack Troops in a time that is crying for such a key battalion. But we have, we may have, one fatal flaw that is ruining, or can ruin, everything. Our loyalty is divided too many ways. The soil is packed with possibilities, but it is infested with other quick-rich cash crops that sap the Oak. Christianity is being cheated by its distant relatives. Before we know it, our Christian oath is subordinate to other controlling interests. In our hearts, where we really have the battle out, we have broken the King of kings to Corporal. Let Him drill the company for an hour Sunday morning, if we feel like it. So, not seeking God first, we seek Him second, then third. And the time quickly comes when we can only find time and money for what is put first. Sooner or later we have to cut back the budget and something has to go, and you and I know what will be first. In life after life the Christian venture is being suffocated by "the thousand and one thorn-like things we have to do this morning." "You cannot serve God and mammon." We won't believe it, and so we smother silently among the cactus.

Life is a garden. But it will "grow up" without our attention. We are here because we need a hoe as much as we need the sun and the rain. To let our thoughts and hopes go unpruned is to take our own life by default. The Christian in most of us is not dying from our evil, but because we won't cut some fairly good things out. "And some seed fell among thorns, and the thorns sprung up and choked them."

"Other seeds fell on good soil and brought forth grain, some a hundredfold."

The seed is so small, the soil so unpromising, the sower seems engaged in a solitary and futile occupation. The world laughs at his labor. Preaching is the last career to consider. Teaching Sunday school is done only under tremendous pressure. The line of applicants is never very long or eager. That seed, they say, has a very low germination rate or childhood is simply the wrong soil for it. The ministry? For many years now that profession has been a humiliating one for the able-bodied. It scarcely deserves a disdainful glance in the mind of the graduate, and his parent. "Why should anyone want to squander his time on a myth when everyone is talking about megatons? No one will listen to you. What the birds miss will scorch on barren rock or be blanketed under best sellers. Just think of all the simply fascinating things you could do. We're splitting atoms now and learning how to swim in space."

And yet the sower finds an ear here and there. Whole sections of the acreage he has painstakingly planted may be a heart-breaking total loss. Yet miraculously, "the fields are white unto harvest." There were some shepherds who stopped to listen, some fishermen who dropped everything to go. "At midday, O King," said Paul to Agrippa, "I heard a voice." "Listen to what gracious words our Lord Jesus Christ saith." Most pay no attention but there are "a happy few."

So the sower goes on sowing, scattering the precious seed on the just and the unjust, high and low, promising and unpromising, not knowing where and when the germ of God may find a spot to root, knowing only that there is always the hope of a crop in every heart, that no man can be stone deaf to the silver tongue of God. Some of nature's soil may seem impossible—forever frozen over like the Arctic, hopelessly solid as a canyon, or permanently barren as desert sand. But the sower goes on, never giving up—there is no human soil but may sometime, given the right conditions, bring forth grain a hundredfold. The Testament has taught him that in the spirit's realm even the climate changes, the skies can clear and sun come out. There in the God-made human elements, water can gush out of rock, the desert can bloom like the rose and "Instead of the thorn shall come up the fir tree."

ONCE when great crowds were accompanying him, he turned to them and said: 'If anyone comes to me and does not hate his father and mother, wife and children, brothers and sisters, even his own life, he cannot be a disciple of mine. No one who does not carry his cross and come with me can be a disciple of mine. Would any of you think of building a tower without first sitting down and calculating the cost, to see whether he could afford to finish it? Otherwise, if he has laid its foundation and then is not able to complete it, all the onlookers will laugh at him. "There is the man," they will say, "who started to build and could not finish." Or what king will march to battle against another king, without first sitting down to consider whether with ten thousand men he can face an enemy coming to meet him with twenty thousand? If he cannot, then, long before the enemy approaches, he sends envoys and asks for terms. So also none of you can be a disciple of mine without taking leave of all his possessions.'

LUKE 14:25-33, New English Bible

✠

'WHEN an unclean spirit comes out of a man it wanders over the deserts seeking a resting-place; and finding none, it says, "I will go back to the home I left." So it returns and finds the house unoccupied, swept clean, and tidy. Off it goes and collects seven other spirits more wicked than itself, and they all come in and settle down; and in the end the man's plight is worse than before. That is how it will be with this wicked generation.'

MATTHEW 12:43-45 (also LUKE 11:25-26), New English Bible

12

An Unfinished Tower
A King's Rash Attack
A Haunted House

"Now great multitudes accompanied him." His unpopularity on trial at the last erases our memory of His recordbreaking popularity on the preaching trail at first. This man brought a country to ramrod attention. Everything He said and did made copy. His fame ran like wildfire. Crowds jammed the streets He took; men climbed sycamores to see Him over the garden of heads; dropped patients through ceilings to get through to Him; and others resigned from the hope of ever talking to Him to take the next hope: "If only I could touch the hem of his garment." People mobbed Him during working hours; men like Nicodemus came by night; He was known to preach with His back to the sea so He could retreat safely by boat. On Good Friday He was deserted to a man, but it looked as if every man lined the streets to sing His praises up through Palm Sunday. It was His spectacular box-office appeal that made the Pharisees mad for blood.

"Now great multitudes accompanied him; and he turned and said to them, 'If any one comes to me and does not hate his own father and mother and wife and children and brothers and sisters, yes, and even his own life, he cannot be my disciple.' " Jesus was not directing husbands to desert their wives, nor requiring that men be criminally negligent of grandparents and children. This was His Oriental way of recruiting soldiers and discharging milksops. Looking out over that sea of faces, He could find few whose heart was in it. The crowd had much in common with one gathered to watch a dogfight or to see Niagara Falls. Here and there He met looks that meant business, but by and large it was a typical Broadway audience that would melt panic-stricken at the first cry of fire. He was searching for words that would break up the "me and my wife and my son John" cliques and shrink the shallow interest down to disciple depth. Here was an impulsive mob spread around Him; He wanted a devoted army under Him. So He used strong language to blow away the chaff that didn't really care to sing, to teach, nor live, nor pray for Him; who wouldn't keep on coming to church if the Communists clamped down or wouldn't risk the ridicule if the campus VIP's turned thumbs down.

So He accentuated the cross. "For which of you, desiring to build a tower, does not first sit down and count the cost whether he has enough to complete it?" "Or what king will march to battle against another king, without first sitting down to consider whether he can win?"

Lately, Christians have been busy covering up the cost. For modern Christianity is a problem of multiplication not subtraction. Prospects are pampered with promises to cushion the shock of the vows. Every comforting bit of available bait is dangled to melt their resistance. "You'll like this church," advertises the hospitality committee, "with its canvass just once a year. Sign here. It won't hurt a bit." The unspoken implication is, "All that is necessary is to put in an occasional appearance and make a nominal pledge. We don't talk about such things as tithing any more, but minimum requirements that entitle you to all the privileges of membership. This will fill in a blank on all your application forms and boost you socially. We can provide far more impressive accommodations for your daughter's wedding and your grandfather's funeral than the Town Hall or the mortuary. Our clergy are much more colorfully robed for those solemn occasions than the justice of the peace or the undertaker. And what would your new neighbors and your child's future college admissions office think if you didn't send him to Sunday school?"

Compared to Christ, suburban congregations seem like kittens playing with a ball of "yearn." We lure prospects. He eliminated them. Membership to us means a catch. To Him it meant a cross. Some visitor saunters in to say: "What has this church to offer?" We hasten to brag about the services. He would challenge: "A yawning crater in the budget, a class without a teacher, a teacher without faith." "Do you folks have a Bible class?" Today's minister makes some lame excuse. Christ would say, "Yes. There is the Bible." And He would pick up any church directory and add: "Here is the absentee class. You are the teacher." A guest reports, "I don't feel welcome here." The Master might reply, "Stay and see that the next visitor does."

He would shake any divinity student loose from superficial study with staggering sentences: "Unless you are prepared to go the whole way don't get in the way." He would shatter the new members as they amble down the aisle: "Halt, who goes there?" "Foxes have holes, and birds of the air have nests; but the Son of man has nowhere to lay his head." "If anyone would come after me let him take up his cross. . . ." The vows of discipleship go deeper than those you made on your wedding day. You must be more faithful to the church than to your wife. You'll have to give up more for this than for your coronary. Reading the Bible isn't enough; praying isn't enough. Attending church isn't enough. "Thou shalt love the Lord thy God with all thy heart, and with all thy soul, and with all thy strength, and with all thy mind"; it involves much more than charity. "And thy neighbour as thyself."

Spelled out for our society it means we must learn how to win enemies and influence friends for Him whose name we are otherwise taking in vain. There is a wilderness of Christian ignorance and superstition in your neighborhood as in your mind and mine. You may be appointed to scout and report. A jungle of "terribly important" activities has sprung up to choke the church. Someone may have to take his reputation into his own hands and help hack out the ensnaring undergrowth. He may have to use his imagination to escape the nauseating stereotyped phrases and obsolete methods, and capsule the news afresh. Someone may be asked to spy for God, to sabotage some of the unfair competition. There may be a call for volunteers who will be brave enough to assassinate propriety. Someone may be needed to help knock the stuffings out of Saturday night before it completely smothers Sunday morning with sleep. Are you sure you want to become a Christian? It might run into money. It could dent one's pile, make us miss a rung up the ladder, wreck the social party system, crash into the way things have always been done.

What a drastic experience joining church could be if a man and his minister actually counted the cost. King Arthur bound his knights, according to Tennyson:

> By so straight vows to his own self,
> That when they rose, knighted from
> Kneeling, some were pale as at the
> Passing of a ghost, some flushed,
> And others dazed as one who wakes
> Half blinded at the coming of a light.

If the men at Arthur's Round Table reeled like that from the effect of the vows of chivalry, what would the awful oath of Christian discipleship do to us if the meaning ever struck us to the soul? It is said to have knocked Paul from his horse and struck him blind.

"For which of you desiring to build a tower, does not first sit down and count the cost, whether he has enough to complete it? Otherwise, when he has laid a foundation, and is not able to finish, all who see it begin to mock him." But why go on about the cost? Why not encourage everyone who will to take the shovel and break Christian ground? Wouldn't it be better to begin than never to join the church at all?

No. Better to take all those not in dead earnest out of the line-up. Christianity cannot accept reckless off-the-cuff commitments. Candidates must deliberately face the hard cold facts about the faith and human nature. It belongs only to those in a "do or die" frame of mind. The lukewarm, the premature, are ineligible.

Actually, this requirement is a protection to each potential member from making a fool of himself. No halfhearted prospect should be permitted at the starting gate. He will look ridiculous running against such second-mile men as St. Francis—what a pitiful spectacle he will make pitching into the ditch as soon as his chest begins to burn! It isn't fair to any entry to minimize the obstacles in the course. Why encourage any hesitant Nicodemus to start something at night he will regret in the light? Christ was brutally frank with every applicant. You have no business in here without the will to win. This is no place to be a dilettante. The bystanders will mock the misplaced, mercilessly.

Any convert who is not half trying also brings dishonor to the whole marathon. The odor of insincerity soon spreads until the business of Christianity reeks with hypocrisy. There are so many fakes cluttering up the cinders, the varsity can't run. The buffoons sporting the Christian insignia in pulpit and pew bring a burlesque atmosphere to the Olympic. A church bursting with deceit instead of heroism brings the whole movement into disrepute and attracts more fraudulence.

This warning to think it over is to be balanced, of course, with the reminder that no one of us knows just who is who. In the talk Jesus made on the Tares, the owner told his hands to hold off weeding until harvest time lest they pull up wheat with the weeds. Only God can tell for sure just which is which and when to weed without unjust injury. Certainly pompous priests and elders have no right to close the doors to anyone who wants in. But our text does arouse prejudice against those who can be talked out of it. The church is open only to the determined for their sake as for herself. Compromise is Christianity's poison.

"Or what king, going to encounter another king in war, will not sit down first and take counsel whether he is able with ten thousand to meet him who comes against him with twenty thousand? And if not, while the other is yet a great way off, he sends an embassy and asks terms of peace."

While Jesus demanded men first figure up what Christianity

was going to exact of them, He also insisted they consider the expenses to which the alternative would put them. It takes something to make a treaty —this kind of peace has its price. Jesus didn't want men swinging jauntily into discipleship, but He didn't want them turning it down without taking a long look to see where that other choice led. Before a man decides the church comes too high, he should get-some competitive bids.

Communism has some clever salesmen, but when all its installments and hidden costs are computed, the total is rather staggering. Who else wants to name his price? A man can sell his soul to his job and let every other claim on his life be subordinate to that first mortgage. It may cost a wife and a few children, plus some other Scrooge-like assessments. He may put his whole trust in his wife. But that may be asking for it. She may not make a very good god. Or a man may negotiate terms with pleasure. But he should look behind the make-up in Hollywood to see what kind of bill that runs up. Don Juan may have missed something. Jesus was not only not afraid of His rivals, He was eager to have a man compare prices.

However, if you don't choose Christianity, you will have to select one of these alternatives. You cannot get away from earth without getting in debt to some god. That is the import of the parable of the unoccupied house.

A man is like a house. Christ is one possible Master of that house. But if Christ is refused, the head chair must soon go to someone else. A vacant estate is a magnet to every footloose trouble that roams by. Any unoccupied soul gets haunted. It is just the squatting place for counterfeiters, bootleggers, a beckoning back alley for every sort of vermin. Unless the windows of a soul are lighted with a durable enthusiasm and the grounds well-kept for that purpose, the rats take over and the weeds grow rank. If God leaves, some devil moves in.

A student prides himself on his open mind—which is a sure sign it isn't. An open mind is a delusion of the footloose. Open minds are in great demand by hungry gods and grabbed up quickly. Someone likes to think he will keep anyone from being master of his house. He will treat a succession of guests courteously, objectively. But the days of that policy are numbered. He is human. He will form attachments. He is vulnerable, he will succumb to someone's sales pitch. He will, just because he is a lonely man, start entertaining some interesting, thrilling visitor too much, and stay up too late. Someone, something, will eventually buy out his estate and run things. If not the Galilean, then Caesar, Marx, or that flourishing American imposter, Success. Hitler was able to take over Germany because it was only nominally Christian. They had become brain worshipers. Alger Hiss and Whittaker Chambers were so proud of their freedom from our religious tradition, they were so objectively liberal, they forgot how hungry human nature is for something to love and serve, and they fell into a communist cell. Chambers' confession forms excellent commentary on this parable. The Soviet faith rushed into his own spiritual vacuum. Every girl knows that a boy will not remain unengaged forever. Jesus saw that was true about his fundamental allegiance. If a man won't bow the knee to Him, then he will sooner or later negotiate with hell's two-faced hierarchy: Venus, Bacchus, Croesus—all thugs in the employ of Beelzebub.

Before becoming Christian, count the cost, lest you make a fool of yourself and make the church a laughingstock. But before you turn it down as too high, make sure you can afford that other choice.

NOW he told a parable to those who were invited, when he marked how they chose the places of honor, saying to them, "When you are invited by any one to a marriage feast, do not sit down in a place of honor, lest a more eminent man than you be invited by him; and he who invited you both will come and say to you, 'Give place to this man,' and then you will begin with shame to take the lowest place. But when you are invited, go and sit in the lowest place, so that when your host comes he may say to you, 'Friend, go up higher'; then you will be honored in the presence of all who sit at table with you. For every one who exalts himself will be humbled, and he who humbles himself will be exalted."

LUKE 14:7-11, Revised Standard Version

✝

HE also told this parable to some who trusted in themselves that they were righteous and despised others: "Two men went up into the temple to pray, one a Pharisee and the other a tax collector. The Pharisee stood and prayed thus with himself, 'God, I thank thee that I am not like other men, extortioners, unjust, adulterers, or even like this tax collector. I fast twice a week, I give tithes of all that I get.' But the tax collector, standing far off, would not even lift up his eyes to heaven, but beat his breast, saying, 'God, be merciful to me a sinner!' I tell you, this man went down to his house justified rather than the other; for every one who exalts himself will be humbled, but he who humbles himself will be exalted."

LUKE 18:9-14, Revised Standard Version

13

The Foot of the Table
The Pharisee and the Publican

DURING A DINNER party Jesus "observed how they picked out the best places." We still are. Children scramble into the car to grab the front seat or fight to be next to the window. Teenagers cling like leeches to the seats along the aisle. But adults covet seats for station as for comfort. Every corporation has its throne room. Churches save the center chair for the chief minister. Colleges carefully arrange the academic procession to suit seniority. Advertisers assume that men itch to be men of distinction and that women don't mind being made May Queen or Miss America. The desire to make the neighbors green with envy has not died out. At least salesmen make that pitch with some success. Age enjoys each sign of respect as young officers flush with pleasure over their first salutes and "Yes, Sirs." It is hard for any of us to be angry with someone who spreads the word that we had a "purple heart" or were graduated *cum laude*. Human nature has not changed, so we still set a speaker's table. And if we do not care so much about seating we do care terribly about "standing." Struggling writers seek status by insisting Americans are all status seekers. And it is status and not chairs that Jesus is talking about in this story.

Which one of us is making much effort to look for a social or professional seat farther down—with less prestige, less fan mail, a smaller office or a less pretentious street address? Name one who is conscientiously working his way to the bottom rung. Ask the minister if he would rather be an assistant minister or take a smaller church. Speakers like to say this country is the home of the common man, but who has ever met one? Men hire attorneys to look up kings not serfs in their ancestry. Steinbeck believes that aristocracy breeds most luxuriantly in a democracy. "You will find best proof of this in America," he writes, "where there is not a single individual who is not descended from an aristocrat, where there is not even an Indian who is not a tribal chief." No one likes to be photographed elbowing his way to the head table, but he won't object to having a little limelight up there with news coverage as near the front page as possible. "Jesus observed how they picked out the best seats."

Then Christ interrupted: "Don't do it." "For every one who exalts himself will be humbled." Jesus pointed to pride as man's deadliest poison and labeled it with His largest red letters. He hated hypocrisy but reserved His roughest language for this peacock streak. The other sins are as flea-bites to pride. She is the mother of vice—the monster that fouled paradise from the first. The serpent hissed this hideous venom to Adam and Eve: "Ye shall be as gods." Milton's Lucifer was ambitious, industrious, virtuous. It was pride that made him devil.

Men talk about sin with a silly grin as if it only had to do with sex or swearing. Sin is rebellion against God. It is run by pride, and it ruins men. Beside pride all the frightening diseases of our day are dandruff. It is pride that jams hell. It is pride that drives men mad for more, crazes them with the idea they deserve more; that says their way is the only way and damns them in the stagnant status quo. It is pride that sours friendship, strangles love, devours faith, blinds men to their need of God and segregates them from their neighbor, fixing them in front of the mirror, and places them in solitary confinement.

The noises that awaken us at night are nothing—nothing but thieves who cannot steal anything that matters, fires that cannot burn what we believe. Pride is the fiend we need to fear. Jesus spent His time casting out fear, except He tried to give men a healthy fear of pride. What pride can do to us should shock us into emergency measures. Pride justifies pallor. Pride goeth before disaster. A jagged piece of rock sticks out of desert sand bearing the arrogant inscription of Ozymandas: "Look on my works ye mighty and despair." Where are they? Buried in dust beside him. If we turn over one of the beatitudes it reads: "Cursed are the proud, for they shall be exiled."

And so He said to us: "When you receive an invitation, go and sit down in the lowest place."

There is nothing yellow about this humility of His. Uriah Heep was not "your 'umble servant" at all, but "a wolf in sheep's clothing." Humility is not being afraid to fight nor falling all over itself to say "Uncle" to everybody. Running away is one thing. Standing by God's ideas is drastically different. What makes us think that bluffing, bullying, beating our way through life to get even, tit for tat, is so brave? Does it not betray butterflies and a craven's heart? Looking God in the face and taking His orders is man's work. No chicken-heart has the courage to go behind his facade and face the frightening list of his failures. No weakling can stand to know the whole truth about himself. Humility calls for that extraordinary valor to take it and step down from the throne in favor of God, pick up a cross, and go to the front and fight for Him. Humility as He handed it on to us never creeps nor crawls. It collapses at the feet of Christ, then crashes into Lucifer's face, armed with the scepter of righteousness. No milksop volunteers for the battalion of Him who dared men to lose their lives to find them.

Where does this humility come from? Not from fear. We note first it comes from knowing how head over heels in debt we are. The proud man sings praises to himself. He is so stuck on himself as to believe he owes everything to the simply marvelous man he is. He smiles smugly and cracks in a loud sunstruck voice, "I'm a self-made man." The humble man traces the source of his successes through himself on back to that teacher who taught him what he knows, to the fathers who fought for his liberty to do it, to the pain-racked mother who went down to the gates of death to give him breath, ultimately to heaven. "Every good gift and every perfect gift is from above."

Humility happens when someone has at last gotten it through his head and heart that a man does not have rights so much as privileges—that the work of his mind and hand is as much more the work of the many minds and hands who made him and mainly of that modest and extravagant Maker who "Giveth to all life, and breath, and all things." "Such knowledge is too wonderful for me; it is high, and I cannot attain unto it." But a glimmer is enough to splatter pride and set us searching for a seat near the foot.

Humility also springs from a sense of sin. No one who thinks he's satisfactory can be humble. It takes knowledge of guilt as well as debt to bring a man to his knees. The Pharisee's pride in his goodness blocked out God. He was so busy congratulating himself he was not like other men, it never occurred to him he was not much like God either. He was so involved in his exercise of spiritual primping that God's glory was entirely lost on him. He was praying before a mirror not a window. He was so tickled at his trickle of tithing, so in love with the way he looked beside the rest, that getting on his knees was all show; inside he felt as if he had swallowed the canary. He was praying neither for help nor pardon but to take the cake.

In cutting contrast to this, off in a corner, another man was on his knees. This man was not comparing himself with the gutter but with the sky. He saw the vast gulf between God and himself. His head was not swelled but bursting with shame for his shortcomings. He smote his breast crying, "God be merciful to me a sinner." It is the moral giant who bows lowest down, not seeking credit but absolution, not aware that he towers over the dwarf but how far short he falls of God. St. Paul said: "Christ Jesus came into the world to save sinners; of whom I am chief." "Why do you call me good?" said the Man among men, "No one is good but God alone." Our guilt, as our debt, breaks a man's pride and sends him to his prayers.

This publican "went down to his house justified, rather than the other; for every one who exalts himself will be humbled, but he who humbles himself will be exalted." We interrupt to ask, "What is so blessed about eating crow and passing up the plums?" Curtain calls are fun.

These prizes shortchange us. Applause is fickle and fleeting and feeds the dying soul on dust. What shall it profit a man though he enters the Halls of Fame? The trophies are tin and soon grow moss.

> The boast of heraldry, the pomp of pow'r
> And all that beauty, all that wealth e'er gave,
> Await alike the inevitable hour:
> The paths of glory lead but to the grave.

What are degrees, medals, to Him who hosts life's banquet? He has promised to turn the tables when He comes. Men bloated on these bribes of honor, who have stuffed themselves with toasts, are but cardboard freaks soon to fly away unhonored and unsung. On that day He will use the devastating words of Christ: "They have their reward." "For everyone who makes himself important will become insignificant." "Give up your seat."

The humble man has forsaken the glory of the grandstand play, given up his rights to right his wrongs. Amid the jangle he hears the eternal music, his mouth dry, not for earth's elixirs, but for the water that maketh a man not to thirst again. Humility is happy here. It makes friends, for the humble man, moved by gratitude does not care to boast nor beat. He has found everything he wants in giving up. And as Buttrick writes: "Heaven bends low to the soul that feels its need."

But humility's finest hour is yet to come. When in some supernatural sense "the meek . . . shall inherit the earth."

So, when you are invited, go and sit in the lowest place, so that on that day when your great host comes at last he may say to you, "Friend, go up higher."

HE said to his disciples, 'There was a rich man who had a bailiff, and he received complaints that this man was squandering the property. So he sent for him, and said, "What is this that I hear? Produce your accounts, for you cannot be manager here any longer." The bailiff said to himself, "What am I to do now that my employer is dismissing me? I am not strong enough to dig, and too proud to beg. I know what I must do, to make sure that, when I have to leave, there will be people to give me house and home." He summoned his master's debtors one by one. To the first he said, "How much do you owe my master?" He replied, "A thousand gallons of olive oil." He said, "Here is your account. Sit down and make it five hundred; and be quick about it." Then he said to another, "And you, how much do you owe?" He said, "A thousand bushels of wheat," and was told, "Take your account and make it eight hundred." And the master applauded the dishonest bailiff for acting so astutely. For the worldly are more astute than the other-worldly in dealing with their own kind.

'So I say to you, use your worldly wealth to win friends for yourselves, so that when money is a thing of the past you may be received into an eternal home.'

LUKE 16:1-9, New English Bible

14

The Dishonest Manager

ONCE UPON A time there was a rich man who had an incompetent manager who was ruining his business, so he fired him. However, while the scoundrel was packing he made some shrewd preparations. He foresaw that he would be too weak to dig and too proud to beg, so when he was cleaning out his desk he called in his master's two delinquent debtors and cut one's debt in half and the other by a fifth. Before walking out into the cold, hard world of unemployment, he took the last minute to make two warm friends.

This is about the boldest parable Christ ever told. But He is not commending that rascal's morals, but applauding his uncommon good sense. This rogue uses his crooked head to get ahead on earth, better than good men use theirs to get to heaven. The man, of course, is a member of the opposition. But Jesus is jealous of this shrewdness for His own side. "For," He said, "the worldly are more astute than the other-worldly in dealing with their own kind."

Take a look first at this fellow's resourcefulness. He is fired, but not floored. He is a good man in an emergency. This parable runs an advertisement for God: "Wanted: *Good* men with this man's business head."

Consider the Connecticut Yankee and his bicycle factory. It will take more than strikes and taxes to put him out of business. Foul weather and flat tires won't keep him from work. A houseful of company can't make him stay home at night if he's needed on the job. Competition doesn't break his spirit; he will make do, think of something, try everything, even to working on Sunday, and he will simply never say "die."

But imagine some Presbyterian excommunicated. He would simply turn over in bed and become Episcopalian or Methodist.

Watch the weather's tyranny over church attendance—it is worse on that than on baseball. House guests literally paralyze Christian production. Saturday night sabotages Sunday morning. This is the way the church died, not with a fight, but a (bad) sniffle.

But see the top salesman under fire. He's too smart for high pressure or fast-talking soapbox tactics. He never stops going to school, never stops studying the consumer mind. No nut is too hard for him to crack. He will enlist the artist, employ the subtlest propagandist, exploit friendship, use flattery, exude charm, open up his home, his bar, even let his customer talk about himself, if it will make a sale.

Compare this to the church's fumbling efforts to "rescue the perishing," or to a typical Christian policy for getting to heaven. Contrast this "all-out" effort of industry with the Sunday school's, or the primitive fumbling approach of a minister calling on prospects. Ministers may not convey the impression that their belief is a matter of life or death to themselves or to anyone else. If one halfhearted attempt won't convert a man, why bother the poor fellow further. Drop a Bible in his lap and leave him alone—"Anyway, I can't take all day." The church gives up where a corporation worth its salt would just begin to fight.

Think of the fervor spent in mastering the fine points of bridge, or improving your golf game. If it takes more coaching, more practice, better clubs, men will spare nothing. They will, as Buttrick suggests, reverently recite the incantations, "Keep your eye on the ball," "Follow through," as if piously intoning some sacred ritual. Jesus is not damning that, but appropriating it for His Cause. No man can get to heaven without equal dedication. It takes something more than a sleepy stab at it to master "the more excellent way." It is not enough to be good. One must be inventive, indefatigable. He must be superior not only in motives but in zeal. He must be good on time, in time. Heaven is not a rest home. It has no room for sluggish saints any more than golf or chess can endure sloppy players. If a man is going to get to heaven, he is going to have to put his mind to it to the same degree it took to land his girl—and a little more. Virtue is worthless unless it is on its toes, intelligent, enthusiastic. Sunday school is not a living death, except by indifference and carelessness. Christ's life was the most exacting adventure ever made—His Cross the most exhaustive experiment.

This dishonest manager has something more that we must have to have heaven—horse sense. If we expect to survive spiritually, we must face the facts as he did to survive physically, as well as steal his fervor.

When he received his notice he did not daydream what might have been, nor pull the wool over his eyes. He became coldly realistic. "What am I to do now. . . ? I am not strong enough to dig, and too proud to beg."

The business world still sets us this good example. It is brutally honest with its figures, basing its decisions strictly on profit and loss. In sharp, sad contrast to this, Christians construct a fool's paradise in their business. Members do not stick to the facts of life Christ offered, but believe what they want to believe and shelve the facts that don't fit in with their preconceived ideas.

Christ labeled pride deadly poison, yet churches still get drunk on pride—and our Alma Mater, our automobile, our place, position (both economic and academic)—can be monuments to pride rather than steps of service. We have casually dismissed the Beatitudes of twenty centuries in favor of a popular little code men like to call "my personal philosophy" which they compiled at odd moments when they were very young, and which they foolishly consume the rest of their lives rationalizing and defending. Christians do not read their manual as frequently as good businessmen read the *Wall Street Journal*. Is it only in pardoning that we are pardoned? In giving that we receive? When have churchmen wrestled with these precepts as fearlessly as merchants struggle with the laws of supply and demand?

The one sure solid fact on which Christ counted was God. Since this was eternally and totally true, He meant more than anything else so He spent much of His time with Him, which is, we say, why His tiny time in public mattered so much for all time. But would it be a blow to a modern minister if he were denied prayer for twenty-four hours? Here is the Book of Life to feed men their daily rations until they are at last freed from the bondage of flesh, but where is the man who would be punished if he couldn't touch a drop of the wine of life for a week? Hell was another fact of His faith. We have pitched it into slang. Nothing could surprise the modern man more than to wake up after death and find out he had to account for his actions to someone besides his wife. The idea that we are under any personal obligation to God has gone out of the universities. And the boys at how many medical and divinity schools are taught by ridicule, which is the most effective brainwash technique known, to smile at the faith as naïve. Which of them feels directly responsible to the Great Physician? "So faith, hope, love abide . . . but the greatest of these is love." Yet love is not often at the top of the list in the hectic life of the church.

The dishonest steward's decision was based on the facts. Christians seldom face up to their dilemma of life and death in the light of truths so sound they still shall stand though everything else pass away. "For the worldly are more astute than the otherworldly. . . ."

In one more respect Christians can emulate shady businessmen. They are superior in foresight as in fervor and fact-facing. Even this shiftless manager used what sunlight was left to make arrangements for the rainy day. This capacity to look ahead is characteristic of this life's clever people. The sponge, of course, does not dig fruitcellars nor store nuts. But the practical Yankee is ready for anything. He anticipates accidents by insurance. He does not stumble into old age unprovisioned —he makes it an attractive haven of benefits. He phones retirement ahead for excellent reservations. He has built a palace for his senior years with his savings.

By comparison with this Scot's strategy the precautions of the elect seem primitive and seedy. The late Joseph Welch claimed that capital punishment accomplishes nothing simply because no man, even waiting on death row, can believe it will actually happen to him. True or false, Christians do not seem to be making plans for their departure with any of the zest they put into preparation for their vacation. Shakespeare said, "All life is a preparation for death," but Americans make of life anything but that. There is preparation for anything up to and including the cemetery lot and legal will, but surely little fuss is made about packing for the beyond. The customary stand on this question was beautifully illustrated by the bard's character, Dame Quickly, that true orphan of the church. When the dying Falstaff whispered he would like a prayer, she shushed him like the fine impractical nurse she was, indicating that he needn't bother himself yet with any such morbid thoughts; so-called Christians, the foolish virgins, don't hold a candle in their practical concern for the new age as compared to the cool calculations of their counterparts in this world for old age. The steward faced his firing into the cold world unflinchingly, and promptly did something about it. This parable recommends that we be just as practical about the new world.

Now what has money to do with celestial arrangements? Why does the New Testament talk more about money than anything else? One-third of His parables, we discover, are devoted to the proper use of possessions. To put it very crudely, this parable is telling us we can bribe paradise with gifts. There are many things money cannot buy, few it cannot have by giving. Now the church has corrupted this idea abominably. We remember particularly the black market in which the church indulged in medieval times on this pretext, that kindled Luther's wrath and ignited the Reformation. But the parable is just as precious.

Getting and spending eventually leaves us bankrupt. It is giving that raises men from the dead. The future belongs to the man who has learned to share. Thrift is superior to prodigality. But immortality is not promised to the thrifty. "For whoever would save his life will lose it. . . ." The prescription is, "And whoever loses his life for my sake, he will save it." The ascent is made by sacrifice. The safest investment is not real estate, it is, if we are to go by the Book, men. The only treasure we shall have in heaven is the amount we have spent here on the men who needed help. There are quack charities—the ditches are filled with rascals playing possum. Beggars cry for crusts that aren't good for them. We must not obey their wishes, nor ours, but God's. But buying stock in eternity is the business of generosity. One is set up in it when he begins lying awake nights, looking for, waiting for, praying for, dying for, someone to whose face he can bring the smile of happiness. Any earnest, honest request will open an account. You will see the man lying there for the first time. He may thirst for your attention as a child abroad craves milk. Your eye may fall on a fertile field in Ethiopia that might not waste money as much as spending it for mink. Whatever you do, if you do it well and as a well-wisher, is going to be ultimately redeemable. Our prosperity or depression above depends on how much we banked below in benevolence.

The mortality rate of this life is not just high, it is 100 per cent. How much time we have left doesn't make any difference. Time, anytime, is short. And in this sense we too have been given our notice as surely as that steward in his story. We can't take our money with us, but it can beat us there by deeds of mercy. They are so sound, He said, it is like building on rock. Why not? It would give us something to look forward to. And when we are forced to leave, it will not be for an unfriendly place. Rather the whole company of our past kindnesses will be over there to welcome us into "eternal tents."

AND *behold, a certain lawyer stood up and made trial of him, saying, Teacher, what shall I do to inherit eternal life? And he said unto him, What is written in the law? how readest thou? And he answering said, Thou shalt love the Lord thy God with all thy heart, and with all they soul, and with all thy strength, and with all thy mind; and thy neighbor as thyself. And he said unto him, Thou hast answered right: this do, and thou shalt live. But he, desiring to justify himself, said unto Jesus, And who is my neighbor? Jesus made answer and said, A certain man was going down from Jerusalem to Jericho; and he fell among robbers, who both stripped him and beat him, and departed, leaving him half dead. And by chance a certain priest was going down that way: and when he saw him, he passed by on the other side. And in like manner a Levite also, when he came to the place, and saw him, passed by on the other side. But a certain Samaritan, as he journeyed, came where he was: and when he saw him, he was moved with compassion, and came to him, and bound up his wounds, pouring on them oil and wine; and he set him on his own beast, and brought him to an inn, and took care of him. And on the morrow he took out two shillings, and gave them to the host, and said, Take care of him; and whatsoever thou spendest more, I, when I come back again, will repay thee. Which of these three, thinkest thou, proved neighbor unto him that fell among the robbers? And he said, He that showed mercy on him. And Jesus said unto him, Go, and do thou likewise.*

LUKE 10:25-37, American Standard Version

15

The Good Samaritan

ONE DAY A city lawyer publicly picked up the hardest question there is and threw it at the country preacher: "What do I have to do to get to heaven?" Instead of squirming, Jesus promptly took the offensive and asked him for his view first. Frustrated but not silenced, the expert repeated an old Jewish recipe: "Thou shalt love the Lord thy God with all thy heart, and with all thy soul, and with all thy strength, and with all thy mind; and thy neighbour as thyself." The Master took him by surprise: "This do, and thou shalt live." Then to keep from looking silly for asking something so simple, the specialist racked his brains for another question and frantically seized upon one that drew from the Master the most famous of all good deeds, except the one He did Himself. This deed was done with words but has done more than deeds to make men dissatisfied with words. Christ took this academic question "Who is my neighbor?" to tell a story that has taught all mankind how to be a good neighbor. Some say it is His masterpiece of parables, and others that it is at least the next to best. But only Luke remembered to write it down. It may be able to save us better than our newest swords.

A certain man was on his way from Jerusalem to Jericho. It was a notoriously thief-infested stretch of rocky mountain road, a long, lonely twenty miles crowded with caves and danger. Jesus and His audience had made the trip many times. The route was perfect for pillage and had been nicknamed "The Bloody Pass." This traveler was ambushed, stripped of everything, beaten to a bloody pulp, and left to die a crimson wreck by the roadside.

Now, just by coincidence, the first man to come by was a priest. He saw the pitiful sight, but didn't stop. The next man was a Levite, literally born to the church. He looked and while no one else was looking, left. Both men were men of God, busy minding their own business with no time nor training to meddle in the lives of men they had never even met. Besides, this was a bloody mess, no telling what disease, and too far gone. And what could one man do out there on that dangerous curve with darkness coming on? A little later the third man arrived. He was a Samaritan. The word was a curse. Samaritans were segregated from Jews as an inferior caste of half-breeds. "The worst thing a Jew could think to call someone was: Samaritan. The only good Samaritan was a dead one." This little story was not spun to a yawning congregation. They were sitting on the edge of their seats with their teeth on edge as the Samaritan stepped up to view the remains. It took daring even to mention him, but to make him hero of the three! Then unbelievably, before this gasping audience, the Samaritan stooped down to see what he could do to save the dying man.

Now, just who is my neighbor? No one knows until he knows. The Samaritan story says, "I don't care who he is." It is the wrong question to ask, for it mistakenly assumes a boundary. The point is not who is your neighbor, but make sure and be one. To whom? Not next door necessarily, but the next necessity you notice. The word "neighbor" has nothing to do with nearness geographically, everything to do with need anywhere you find it—wherever you hear it calling you.

The first thing that makes the Samaritan our model neighbor is good eyes. A man has to be looking for trouble to find it. He has to have his mind on another to notice when he stumbles, to know enough about him to know what he needs. Men can't wait to tell someone everything they know—but there's no room in such a conversation to spill their problem. Hospitality takes vision and watchfulness.

And the Samaritan was able to see one man at a time. He broke up the mob rule that wrecks neighborhoods by classifying men as communist, condemning them as Democrats, and says so-and-so is not a man who happens to be black but a "nigger" first and last, or "he's rich," as if that said everything there was to say about him. And by that blanket category men are blinded to the individual mortal man, distinguished by some special value, each one a unique wreck of grief. But we coffin them as hopelessly alcoholic, hopelessly happy, hopelessly poor. Like the flophouse bum, they are all then typed beyond our influence. We turn away from them then as though they were already dead men, as the priest and Levite did. But the Good Samaritan tore through the mass of averages to a man who needed help.

Our good neighbor's next move was to get personal. Of course, goodness must be organized today in a world where everything is organized from crime to pleasure. But goodness at its best must depend mainly on doing things "first class." That added line in ink is what makes a Christmas card. This story is a sharp reminder that not every cry for help that comes to our attention should be treated as a case for an institution. Some men are too proud to refer, defer, to a superior. They have all the answers. Many, however, delegate everything to an agency. The Samaritan did not turn over his man to the police station in Jericho. He did not flag the next man, appoint a committee, or ship his patient to a hospital. He relied completely on his own good will. How many casualties are mistakenly sent to any psychiatrist by irresponsible friends? The rest home may not be a kindness, but an "out." "All right, all right, I'll get you an appointment," but the man wants someone to talk to *now*. "Don't register me with an office with its interminable red tape, its irrelevant applications and insulting waiting rooms." The cry is now to *you*—to someone who can spare a time. One of the most precious things about the Samaritan was simply this: he employed no mechanical grappling hook. He did not take down the man's name and serial number to add to his mailing list for holiday fruitcakes. He got down on his knees in the dirt beside the bleeding form and dressed the wounds with his own hands. He actually poured on the oil and wine, put him on his own beast and took him to the inn all by himself. The deed was born of desperation a bit, but the sick need mothering as well as medication and his home-made help included that and said "get well soon" more convincingly than the chaplain's routine card. How awful to be attacked in that desolate spot in pre-penicillin night! Yes and no. For all the competence of miracle drugs, the Samaritan did something that impersonal hospitals named after him cannot do with their faces cautiously masked both in and out of the operating room. The sterile field can go too far, and be a heartless tomb.

The Angel of Mercy in this man was flexible. He didn't determine artificially just when he would do a good deed. No doubt he had made his pledges for the year and would visit the orphans Monday and see shut-ins Saturday. But he had the capacity to take advantage of an opportunity when it turned up. A knock at the door catches men off guard. But who knows when he'll meet the ditched man? The Samaritan didn't tell the poor wretch he would take care of everything on his way back through. Christian kindness is quick to jump to its feet. And in Christian courtesy there can be no cold professional condescension—"I'll help you when I get good and ready"; it is always ready and good. "I have the honor to be your servant." The good neighbor must be adjustable, interruptable, prepared when he is not prepared.

In fact it takes sacrifice to make a neighbor. The Samaritan's business in Jericho was presumedly just as pressing as the priest's. It had to wait. We can't guess what it cost him—with this kind of man it didn't matter, too much. His schedule was shot. Perhaps he missed his caravan. It cost him something in oil and wine for first aid and in precious time and money to locate and pay an inn to put him up. But the largest expense was giving himself.

There was danger in it too. Was the man diseased? Violent? Was he put there as bait by men hiding just behind those rocks? The story points up the element of danger in every good deed that ever was. The danger to your reputation: "Whom did I see you with the other night?" "Yes, I know her heart is breaking, but who would believe that, under all that paint?" Yet Jesus stayed with the scarlet woman at the well. To be kind to the unstable takes uncommon trust, which makes one vulnerable. Trying to be understanding exposes one to every kind of rebuff, ridicule, misunderstanding, and very often, resentment. Goodness could not exist without bravery.

But the Samaritan did not try to play God—just to be a good man. We are not asked to put everyone we are asked to help all the way through school. Not every cry we hear will become a permanent assignment. Only a cup of water may be called for, one meal missed. This philanthropist didn't move his case to Samaria nor take over his life. He did his turn and departed. He was not desperate to purchase some parasite to lean on him. "Do-gooders" can hunt down someone to groan out thanks after thanks to feed his helper's ego. Christians are asked only to do what they can. Obviously we are not doctors, not billionaires, not God. So the Samaritan did not take on the complete rehabilitation of this poor fellow—he left something for the innkeeper to do. Here was not only a good man, but a man good enough to believe that other men were good and would carry on after he did what he could.

But his deed does feature a second-mile attraction. The mark of his goodness was that he did not do the least he could do. His help was heaped up—not just enough but a little extra. He was "pouring on oil and wine" when he dressed the wounds and didn't dump the man at the inn. He made arrangements for repairs. He didn't have to do that to go down in history. We see him standing there by his beast as he was about to leave the next morning, leaving some more money. And he couldn't help saying, as he said goodby, "I'll pay you whatever more." This man was thorough. Think of our feeble stabs and starts at goodness; this was a finished performance. We get the impression as he rode away that he liked doing his good deed—not for the credit, for perhaps the man was still unconscious, and was never to see his saviour. Goodness is an art of modest extravagance and loving care.

What must I do to obtain eternal life? Nothing will work if you go at it that way. If you help because you have to, it won't help. Goodness always goes beyond the line of duty spontaneously. That's what it means. It is, whatever else, more than "my fair share." It is the something more you can't help doing. It is, and always will be, a royalty of mercy.

And goodness not only takes us there, but lingers after us here longer than anything else. To say men never forget a slight is not quite true. They do. It is love that is eternal and hardest for time to erase. Men will forget our failings, even our profession; they will not soon forget their good neighbors. We do not know what extremely important errand took the Samaritan to Jericho that day—Luke couldn't even remember his occupation, if Jesus ever gave him one. But the world has not forgotten in all of two thousand years the little thing he did en route.

When this story was finished for the very first time, Jesus turned to what we think was a little different lawyer and said, we believe, gently: "Which of these three, thinkest thou, proved neighbor unto him that fell among the robbers?" And staring at his feet in shame and touched, for all his prejudice (as we have been every time we hear it told), the lawyer said: "He that showed mercy on him." And the Master, who must have been thinking of men like us who would, long after, question Him as did this lawyer, recommended something very practical which we can't help but think applies right now: "Go, and do thou likewise."

IV

This Is Your Life

ONE of the multitude said to him, "Teacher, bid my brother divide the inheritance with me." But he said to him, "Man, who made me a judge or divider over you?" And he said to them, "Take heed, and beware of all covetousness; for a man's life does not consist in the abundance of his possessions." And he told them a parable, saying, "The land of a rich man brought forth plentifully; and he thought to himself, 'What shall I do, for I have nowhere to store my crops?' And he said, 'I will do this: I will pull down my barns, and build larger ones; and there I will store all my grain and my goods. And I will say to my soul, Soul, you have ample goods laid up for many years; take your ease, eat, drink, be merry.' But God said to him, 'Fool! This night your soul is required of you; and the things you have prepared, whose will they be?' So is he who lays up treasure for himself, and is not rich toward God."

LUKE 12:13-21, Revised Standard Version

16

The Man God Called a Fool

"THE LAND OF a rich man brought forth plentifully." So far this story could be told on any one of us. Each man may reserve the word "rich" for another man with more—as Mellon may have saved it for Rockefeller—but in this peasant preacher's Near Eastern eyes, even the American Working Man would easily deserve the title. You and I are rich beyond the wildest dreams of most men on earth—rich in groceries with freezers full of fresh vegetables right out of the garden in January, rich in health with magic immunity, miracle medicines and fabulous hospitals filled with Florence Nightingales for T.L.C. We are rich in hundreds of gasoline horses faster and far more comfortable than any camel—rich in houses with huge staffs of mechanical servants to do the laundry and the dishes and furnish whatever weather we wish inside. This parable begins with a little bit of our own autobiography. "The land of a rich man brought forth plentifully."

What's wrong with that? Nothing. It is no sin to be prosperous as it is no virtue to be poor. Rags can result from laziness as easily as riches can be robbed. The starving man may be more selfish than the one who fills his garbage cans.

In fact, America could not have been made without money. It took possessions to produce civilization. A faithful husband had to have his private cave, his own club, and regular hunting ground to get enough ahead to have time to think and invent. The conquest of the chaotic mind as well as primitive political conditions was made, not by Tarzans in the trees, but by men of means. And the backbone of every religious reform has not been itinerant beggars, but successful businessmen. Today the Christian church is not carried on by the destitute but by the Affluent Society.

And despite the raging economic prejudice, Jesus never condemned wealth. His followers were not penniless—frugal perhaps, but not Franciscan. His recommendation to the Rich Young Ruler was not wholesale advice to everyone, no order for civilization to sell out—that counsel was an individual prescription for one personal problem. And Christ's shining hero, the Good Samaritan, was surely well-to-do, at least he had plenty to pay for another's keep and credit too to promise the Keeper of the Inn to cover any further bills. The Roman Officer who, He said, had more faith than any man He'd ever seen in Israel, had many servants and much goods. The homes of Mary and Martha and Peter where He sometimes stayed were not slums. And He was often asked to dinner by wealthy men like Simon the Pharisee. Zaccheus and Matthew, two of His men, were tax collectors—sure moneymakers in those days. He was born in a barn, but it was there three kings were said to open their treasures to Him. He was a peasant's son, but descended from David the King. He knew how to fast, but believed in "eating and drinking" so much that critics called Him "glutton, winebibber." The Nazarene never took any vows of poverty Himself. The robe He was wearing near the end was fine enough for soldiers to gamble over and He was laid at the last in the lovely tomb of a wealthy friend.

But when a rich man comes to the question, as every American must, "What shall I do with my money?" Jesus marked it: "Handle with extreme care." We say, "Watch, so it won't slip through your fingers." He branded it radioactive and cried, "Beware lest it eat into your soul." Money is not the root of all evil, it is "the love of money." It is all right for a man to have things, but not right for things to have a man. If one takes Christian precautions money can't hurt, but if one is spiritually careless, money can devour him. To have something is to have a fire. "Much goods" menaces as well as prospers. We should thank God for more but not fail to post a stronger guard against it.

This parable catches an honest man in the act of being

executed by his own estate. He may have made money hand over fist, but he made it fair and square. There was no odor about how he earned it. It was where he thought it came from and what he did with it that made it spoil on his hands and heart.

First he was immature enough to make believe that his belongings were really his. The sickening words, "I, my, mine," appear twelve times in this tiny tragedy. It never occurred to him that anyone else had anything to do with his success. His mind was so jammed with what he had done and paid for, he couldn't consider the crowd of others who taught him all he knew and earned him what he had. The facts that the weather worked his way and the ground grew bumper crops were somehow twisted in his insanity to his credit, and not to what healthier men have insisted is the Providence of God. He lost his head, not to disease, but to his ego and raved on unnoticed in the popular chorus of human delirium.

When his ship came in he did not see the hand of God, so could not see why he should share the cargo with the rest of God's unfed children. He selfishly assumed his surplus was his, with no strings attached, to salt away. Heaven rained on him, so he naïvely thanked himself and dammed it up. "I will pull down my barns, and build larger ones; and there I will store all my grain and goods."

Some might applaud him for playing safe. God called him a fool for taking a chance. First, because it was no sooner said than God said, "This night," and he was dead. Perhaps in the frantic push to put up barns he lost his health. When he was ready to retire and live off the accumulated fat, his time was up. His death is no mystery to be solved; he simply burned himself out getting ready for the rainy day. His funeral was no surprise but carried out exactly according to his selfish will. He had been dialing the undertaker for years by his folly. Someone has suggested that a minister may have intoned over his grave, "Forasmuch as it hath pleased God," but his death did not please God. The man died because he was a fool. He had deliberately blown out his candle with the whirlwind of his greed.

But the tragedy was not the poor wretch's untimely dispatch. Sooner or later every man loses his life, and the Galilean who got the most out of life had little of it. But death is not the disaster. The disaster is to go to hell. This man was a fool for selling his soul.

Because he tried to be practical instead of righteous, life played its old practical joke on him. He got paid in bacon instead of stars. He got grain by the barnload without any music. Hoarding takes up time and space, so he had to give away his generosity, his imagination, his conscience—and at last get rid of God and hand over all of heaven to have his chunk of earth. He made his bed in that business until he was bred for that business only, until heaven would have bored him to death. He lost his life to make a livelihood. He failed to keep the recommended distance between who he was and what he had, and it killed him body and soul.

"And the things you have prepared, whose will they be?" He was so sure that his best-laid plans were made not with some uncertain, unseen, and hazy heaven in mind, but built on earth's solid ground. He was insured to the hilt for his senior years so he could "Eat, drink, be merry." Here was one smart fellow who would not be fooled into waiting around for some imagined piece of pie in the sky. He would get paid right here and now in sensual cash. "But God said to him, 'Fool! This night your soul is required of you.'" The man was mad. Many do not know it, for earth is a madhouse crowded with his kind. It seemed so sensible a thing to do. But that monkey-business is building on sand. That man's invitation to Paradise arrived that very night, but he was not ready. He had no faith nor interest in such a prospect. He was dressed inside and out for a carnival.

This parable is very sad, but sad to shock us into happiness —to make us stop and take stock as the shadows lengthen over our lives. I think it is agreed that Americans are not so bad.

But the question this story raises is not are we good or evil, but are we fools squandering eternity for a pocketful of pleasure?

Someone cared enough about you and me to hand on this story and finally hand over His life to keep us from acting the fool. He was not afraid to bring up the subject of money over and over; it was for our sake He said, "Provide yourselves with purses that do not grow old, with a treasure in the heavens that does not fail."

'But what do you think about this? A man had two sons. He went to the first, and said, "My boy, go and work today in the vineyard." "I will, sir", the boy replied; but he never went. The father came to the second and said the same. "I will not", he replied, but afterwards he changed his mind and went. Which of these two did as his father wished?' 'The second', they said. Then Jesus answered, 'I tell you this: tax-gatherers and prostitutes are entering the kingdom of God ahead of you. For when John came to show you the right way to live, you did not believe him, but the tax-gatherers and prostitutes did; and even when you had seen that, you did not change your minds and believe him.'

MATTHEW 21:28-32, New English Bible

17

The Deceitful Sons

IT TOOK COURAGE for Jesus to cleanse the temple, but it took more to go back to the temple the next time. That created a crisis which He handled with this parable. As soon as He came in the door and started to teach, "the chief priests and the elders" rudely interrupted with these menacing words: "By what authority are you doing these things, and who gave you this authority?" Since Jesus held no political or religious office, they wanted to know what gave Him the right to attack the temple personnel in such a shocking and brutal manner. The temple staff was surrounding Him, still stinging from His rough handling the last time He was there. He would do well to get away easily. No wonder this was the week Jesus would lose His life. Men were waiting with stones to make Him eat His words. Now was the time to back down if He wanted to save His skin for a long, successful ministry. He was young, and the writer of Hebrews insisted, "was in all points tempted like as we are." His mouth must have been dry and this decision difficult. But He stood His ground—He was good at thinking on His feet.

"Jesus answered them, 'I also will ask you a question; and if you tell me the answer, then I also will tell you by what authority I do these things.' " He was thinking fast, fighting for time. " 'The baptism of John, whence was it? From heaven or from men?' " This stroke of sheer genius and raw courage must have won the grudging admiration of His enemies. In any case it gained time and put them not only on the defensive but into complete chaos. "And they argued with one another, 'If we say, "From heaven," he will say to us, "Why then did you not believe him?" But if we say, "From men," we are afraid of the multitude; for all hold that John was a prophet.' " Finally, after a humiliating struggle with themselves, they were forced to give up in front of everyone. It was a lie: "We do not know." And their failure let Jesus get away: "Neither will I tell you by what authority I do these things."

But Jesus could not let them get away with religious murder red-handed. Their refusal to answer about John exposed their fundamental insincerity. If they would not answer, He would have to answer for them. But His parable was not a stone but an appeal. The story was told to show them up to themselves and by shame and warmth to make honest men of them.

It was the same old story. "A man had two sons." His God was not pretentious or complicated. The word is big enough to satisfy the whole family of man, literate and illiterate, young and old. This word does not mean He is anthropomorphic, but that it is the best word we have. He is out beyond it somewhere, but, by the extension of this domestic avenue, available to both the disillusioned philosopher and the innocent child. God has two sons, not a large family—for Him—but that is enough to take in everybody. These two boys are all He has, and they are as different as night and day, and yet they are identical twins in deceitfulness.

The father approached the first son and said: " 'My boy, go and work today in the vineyard.' 'I will, sir,' the boy replied; but he never went. The father came to the second and said the same. 'I will not,' he replied, but afterwards he changed his mind and went. Which of these two did as his father wished?" " 'The second,' they said." They answered right, for they were like the first son.

Those religious people, the "Pillars of the Church," were notoriously guilty of not keeping their promises to God. "For when John came to show you the right way to live, you did not believe him." Jesus was not blaming them for not following Jesus, but for not following the best example of their own tradition. John preached the stern, ascetic philosophy they professed, but they were not John. For John believed every word of it, and they only *said* they did. John gave his life for his faith, and they gave their faith to their life. They intoned the words piously, but without the steps to back it up. "This people honors me with their lips, but their heart is far from me."

Of course, hypocrisy is always the hazard of religion, stalking hard on the heels of every professing person. God can use man, and that is what religion is for, but tragically man uses God. Religion is our hope, but it is very dangerous because of this peril of insincerity. A man no sooner makes up his mind to follow God than he is besieged by the temptation merely to flatter Him instead. So the temple has always been filled with suitably dressed, legally acceptable, and superficially loyal imposters. This kind of religion includes preaching, the repetition of promises week after week. It means everything remotely connected with religion, and the more remote the better, everything except action which is religion's main business. The hypocrite can take over the pulpit, monopolize the pew, drown out others with his hymns and prayers. He never forgets to say "Amen" at the right time and with just the right inflection. He is completely at home in the ecclesiastical atmosphere, and unrelenting before God. His religion is a form, a routine. It is not dynamic and growing, but static, empty. He is very particular about the way he worships but it does not have its way with him. He makes a few good-looking sacrifices to get away without having to make "the sacrifice of God . . . a broken and a contrite heart." His faith has crystallized. It is a tomb in which he is burying himself.

He said, "I tell you this: tax-gatherers and prostitutes are entering the kingdom of God ahead of you. For when John came to show you the right way to live, you did not believe him, but the tax-gatherers and prostitutes did." Both boys were two-faced. But the second boy, the prodigal, though he began by saying "No," ended up by doing it. The bad boy finally obeyed, but the good boy used goodness to disobey. The good boy was good to himself, for himself, not for God. His was a goodness in name and appearance only, but it was a goodness used against God, the best way to get away from Him. It was not godliness, it was a goodness the devil made. The bad boy was not so bad as to be good for a bad reason. He was not guilty of pretended goodness. He never brought his crime as a fifth column into the church. He was guilty from weakness, not from design. It is easier for honest evil to reform than dishonest virtue.

However, Jesus is not praising prostitution and downright dishonesty. He was making this speech and addressing this parable to the Pharisees; it was never addressed to the prodigals. For the Pharisee's sake He was saying that rebellion was not so insidious and fatal as the sin of betrayal. He was not excluding the insincere forever from paradise, only remarking that it would take longer for them to reform than for the prodigal. This story does not whitewash the confessed sinner. Christ would be the first to explain to prodigals that the race to heaven will be close.

But the sin of insincerity sharply stamps this second son today. The unchurched have been taking advantage of Christ's warning to the churched. It is a common trick today for the prodigal to excuse himself with Christ's aversion to the Pharisee. "Of course, I'm a sinner; do you think I want to be sitting with those other hypocrites in church?" But there is nothing admirable about being a black sheep and nothing worse than being proud of it. This "disillusion of grandeur" so prominent today in the prodigal is the very vice of the Pharisee. The modern prodigal is often a Pharisee too, proud of his wickedness. The prodigal has lost the charm of shame he had for Christ. Jesus could not bear the first boy's pride and exploitation of goodness. But the second boy has now sunk to a pride and exploitation of evil. What could be worse to Christ than the prostitutes and tax collectors who had become Pharisees, flaunting their dissipation. This is a new and far more insidious form of hypocrisy.

But the key question has not changed. "Which of these two did as his father wished?" That question cuts through every ruse used to camouflage the business of life. The twentieth century is proud of what it knows and bestows its highest honors on learning. The first question the college admission board asks is, "What were your grades in high school?" Jesus asks every student this slightly different question: "Who did the will of his father?" It is important to know, for instance, all there is to know about Christianity. And seminaries ask endless examination questions to see what ministerial students know about everything that has ever been written on the subject. But Christ would ask the graduating class: "Which one did the will of his father?" We sanctify success and show it with salary and promotion. The minister himself is measured by the size of his congregation. But the right question to ask is: "Which one did the will of his father?" Men select their Miss America, Fulbright, Pulitzer, and Nobel prize winners. Christ would say, "Yes, yes," but "Which of these did as his father wished?" St. Paul said that of all the Christian virtues the three most important were faith, hope, and love. This parable reminds us, however, that they are grown only from obedience. The first word the Bible says to us is "God." The last word the Bible says to us, and without which the whole Book is wasted on us, the last word is "Go!" And according to this story, the first word we shall hear in heaven is not "Which version did you use?" but "Which one did?"

A T that very time there were some people present who told him about the Galileans whose blood Pilate had mixed with their sacrifices. He answered them: 'Do you imagine that, because these Galileans suffered this fate, they must have been greater sinners than anyone else in Galilee? I tell you they were not; but unless you repent, you will all of you come to the same end. Or the eighteen people who were killed when the tower fell on them at Siloam—do you imagine they were more guilty than all the other people living in Jerusalem? I tell you they were not; but unless you repent, you will all of you come to the same end.'

He told them this parable: 'A man had a fig-tree growing in his vineyard; and he came looking for fruit on it, but found none. So he said to the vine-dresser, "Look here! For the last three years I have come looking for fruit on this fig-tree without finding any. Cut it down. Why should it go on using up the soil?" But he replied, "Leave it, sir, this one year while I dig round it and manure it. And if it bears next season, well and good; if not, you shall have it down."'

LUKE 13:1-9, New English Bible

✙

'SUPPOSE one of you has a servant ploughing or minding sheep. When he comes back from the fields, will the master say, "Come along at once and sit down"? Will he not rather say, "Prepare my supper, buckle your belt, and then wait on me while I have my meal; you can have yours afterwards"? Is he grateful to the servant for carrying out his orders? So with you: when you have carried out all your orders, you should say, "We are servants and deserve no credit; we have only done our duty."'

LUKE 17:7-10, New English Bible

18

The Unproductive Fig Tree
The Servant's Duty

PALESTINE IS NOT a Dead Sea now and never was. The barbed wire
and the machine guns cutting up the country today tattle
on its powder-keg character ever since Abraham first moved in.
Jesus lived in the middle of this chronic turbulence, while
Rome was still there. And this parable was produced from some
bloody mess that Pilate made. The ingredients of that disaster
were Galileans, and some busybodies had just broken this de-
licious news to Jesus. The bearers of these bad tidings assumed
that the victims of that calamity must have had it coming to
them or they would never have been in it. They stood there
pointing their superior fingers at this hideous massacre as an
act of God against the guilty. In ignorance and egotism these
men were true sons of Job's Comforters.

Jesus could not bear their pedestal and attacked it with
devastating candor and compelling genius. "Do you think," He
said, "that these Galileans were worse sinners than all the other
Galileans, because they suffered thus? I tell you, No; But unless
you repent you will all likewise perish." We cannot condemn
any groaning Job just because Nature or human nature picks
on him. There often is a strong relationship between suffering
and someone's sin, and frequently "accidents" can be seen coming long before they arrive; but the volcano, like the summer
shower, rains on the just and the unjust alike. Even if Nature
on the rampage works for God, it does so in mysterious ways
we cannot possibly understand. In any case, who are we to talk?
Any tragedy is a judgment on the bystanders as much as on those
it struck. The Master meant that the survivors deserved the
punishment every bit as much as the dead. "And unless you

repent," He added, "you are going to get the same treatment." The words were hard and only too clear, but He needed an exceptionally good illustration to cinch this age-old argument and to pardon the offense of His stinging condemnation. We must remember, too, these words were speaking to condescending pride—specifically to take some very self-important persons down a peg.

"A man had a fig tree planted in his vineyard; . . . and he said to the vinedresser, lo these three years I have come seeking fruit on this fig tree, and I find none. Cut it down. Why should it use up the ground?" That fig tree never did anything wrong. It was perfectly harmless shade, but it never had any figs on it, and it was in the way, stealing sun and space from something useful. God puts people on His planet for the same reason a farmer plants trees—for a purpose. And Israel made Jesus think of that sterile fig tree. It was God's favorite, the only plant of its kind on the whole plantation. He had high hopes for it, and had spent hours, years, generations of work on it. He had sacrificed patriarchs, judges, kings, and prophets, to get out of Israel what He had put into her, only to get in deeper with each additional investment. The tree had been terribly expensive in buried talents and unprofitable patience. It was the privileged apple of His eye and He had waited on it hand and foot. "When Israel was a child, then I loved him, . . . I taught Ephraim also to go, taking them by their arms; . . . I drew them with cords of a man, with bands of love: . . . How shall I give thee up. . . ?" But what had come of all that tender loving care and precious time and space? Nothing. We can only guess at God's reluctance to let Israel go. We only know He waited longer than He should when He finally said: "Cut her down."

At the last minute, someone said: "Wait!" Christ and postponement came from His other hand. "Leave it, sir, this one year while I dig round it and manure it. And if it bears next season, well and good; if not, you shall have it down." And God gave in. Just as Moses earlier had talked Him into giving them a little more time, so Christ won a last chance to coax that old tree into production.

This parable is a piercing alarm, for it pronounces His nation's doom and in the same breath announces a stay of execution. Israel's crisis had come. The emergency called for radical surgery—which explains the severity of this parable. By rights, Israel's time was up, but by the mercy of God she was, figuratively speaking, granted "one year more" to make up her mind and come across with the fruits the planter had every right to expect. It was now or never. But the Jews slept on, dead to the world they were designed to serve. Next year at harvest time was the same old story—no figs. And Israel as a spiritual force was through.

That failure does not make this parable obsolete. It solicits the United States now as Israel then. If the doom of Jerusalem as the body politic seemed imminent in Jeremiah's day, how many frightening sounds indicate something is sawing at the foundations of our future? The deadly "mushrooms" that can shoot up overnight should be enough to convince us that anything could happen.

The parable speaks on behalf of the entire Bible, not merely for itself. Nations rise and fall at the beck and call of the Almighty. They do not give birth to themselves nor live long because they are smart. God is both midwife and Master in His own house. Twenty some civilizations have already been killed, not by bad luck nor by some bully next door, but basically because God wouldn't put up with their insolence and sterility any longer. Let superficial historians hassle as they will, the Book already has its mind made up—nations are permitted on the stage of history only so long as they serve the purposes and enjoy the patience of the Lord of history. Where is the Holy Roman Empire now? France is a shadow of her former self. England has had her "finest hour." Who's next? God has His reasons for putting an Empire together, and when it will no longer play into His hand, He has to let it drop.

Our beloved country was born believing it was the child of

God, convinced it was going somewhere for His sake. "Our pilgrim fathers by the light of the smoking lamp on the *Mayflower*, before landing at Plymouth inserted these words into the Mayflower Compact. 'We whose names are underwritten have undertaken for the glory of God to establish in Virginia the first colony for the advancement of the Christian faith.'" The prayers of George Washington that awful winter at Valley Forge and of Lincoln during the dark bloody hours of disunion promise something more than this country's survival; some bigger national purpose than the pursuit of our own happiness breathes in our official documents. We are now engaged in a death struggle with an enemy to everything we hold dear. Like Lincoln, in those heart-rending days a century ago when brother slaughtered brother, we do not know what else to do than to arm to the teeth. But there is one thing about which there can be no mistake. If our beloved land lives to see the light of day dawning a century away, it will not be merely because we were the best bomb makers the world has ever seen, but because somehow, even during this depression, we were able to make God a profit. We are on trial right now, privileged as Israel never was. God has every right to expect of us a bumper crop of Christian fruit.

But all the things that have happened in the last few years are enough to make us believe that He is not too happy with our yield so far. Are we known abroad as the servant of the Lord? Would our national neighbors agree that we have been true to our Pilgrim Fathers' aim: "The advancement of the Christian faith"?—or do we spend more on beer and coke? Does our mission field speak louder than Madison Avenue? Do our brothers overseas know us best by our hospitals or by Hollywood? Perhaps we spend more time getting people to buy things they don't need here than in philanthropy there. We talk about our wonderful way of life, and we should. But our crammed courtrooms, and our gory newspapers, and our televised chatterboxes in the corner (with its slapstick drama and the flesh and blood dressed in vacant gum-chewing stares) are a humiliating exposure of America's interest level.

It does not take too much imagination to believe that we are living on borrowed time. And there is enough evidence to make us worry that our nation could be carried off the stage of history, not bleeding to death from nuclear wounds but inside from egotism and self-service. How will the archaeologist read the epitaph of the Americans? "The Almost Chosen People," as one title has it? Or will we manage in the blood-curdling distractions of television thrillers and international terror to keep "this nation under God" and "be true to Thee till death"? Surely this old earth is holding its breath to see what we are going to do next. From God's point of view, it remains to be seen whether this planet can produce anything more promising than those poisonous "mushrooms," engulfing and fatal. God did not plant His fig tree to get fungi. Our existence hangs as surely as Israel's did on whether we can produce godliness in large enough quantities to bring down to earth His dreams of a Kingdom.

The Christian church is taking the examination now the synagogue failed. But see the wreck of Christendom. It has been divorced from itself—Rome from Protestantism—for four centuries. It has splintered into hundreds of denominations, sects, and orders, seldom seeming like sisters of the same family to others or toward each other. What are we coming to? Can we achieve unity without suicidal uniformity or coercive bureaucracy? These are problems which with man are impossible. But do we go on sleeping like innocent babes while the world dies waiting for the followers of Christ to be friends again? Must the church fight organized crime, and Lucifer's smoothly running divisions of materialism with childishly crude guerrilla warfare? Will it ever get moving "like a mighty army"? "You have one year more."

Each of us must be man enough to take the parable personally. We have plane crashes in Chicago now and communist brain wash instead of Pilate mixing the blood of men with animals. But our disasters, just as those in other days, carry bet-

ter men than we are to their flaming deaths. They are shocking
reminders not of our safety but of the danger we are in unless
we act quickly. Tragedies are to make us ask questions. "What
is our excuse for living in the eyes of God? What did we do
yesterday or intend to do today that justifies our oxygen intake?"
Or are we taking up room here unnecessarily in irrelevant sweat?
This story shakes from each of us the crucial question: "Am I
doing what God sent me here to do?" This parable is not a sooth-
ing Sunday vesper chime, but a desperate blast on the trumpet to
get us to our feet, to get us to fight for God like men, not animals;
to get us to do something constructive—"all by myself"—in our
families, as well as church members and citizens, before it is
too late. We read in the morning paper of the bloody deaths of
other men, and then we read the meaning in the Book: "Unless you repent you shall all likewise perish." "Ask not for whom
the bell tolls, it tolls for thee."

The parable of the servant's duty is apropos here. Once again,
Christ "is cruel to be kind." Unlike most of the parables, this
one does not grow out of the context. Dr. Bruce believes that
after writing his Gospel, Luke had this story left over "in the
bottom of his portfolio," and decided the seventeenth chapter
was the place to put it.

"Suppose one of you has a servant ploughing or minding
sheep. When he comes back from the fields, will the master say,
'Come . . . and sit down?' Will he not rather say, 'Prepare my
supper, . . . then wait on me while I have my meal; you can
have yours afterwards'?" God makes a bad first impression in
this. This makes Him sound like a slave-driver instead of an
understanding employer. But that is only one side of the story
and one side of God.

This parable is an attempt to explode the kind of religion
Jesus saw flourishing around Him. The typically religious men
were not acting like bankrupt sinners at all but were putting on
airs, wearing condescending smiles, and acting as if their religious dues were all paid up. They behaved as if they had done
all the work they were hired to do. They had kept the com-

mandments and offered neatly balanced ledgers. They had done their share, so God now owed them a special place in the sun.

Jesus' parable proves that God doesn't owe us a thing. God owns us outright, "It is he that hath made us and not we ourselves." Everyone knows what a slave is and whom he belongs to. And a slave knows his place. This parable uses that familiar relationship to plot our exact position toward God. Whatever God cares to give us is up to Him; there is nothing coming to us. Our merit is a minute in God's eternity. We can take no credit for the world, for our own brainstorms, opportunities. We are even indebted to Him for our determination and our energy to do right. Everything we do to thank God only adds to our debt, for even our thanks is borrowed. If we give Him our life we are only letting Him have what already belongs to Him. No man could possibly go beyond the line of duty to God. For when saints and martyrs have given up everything, suffered, and at last laid down their lives, they must look up into their Maker's face and admit in all honesty: "We are servants and deserve no credit; we have only done our duty."

But, "Happy that servant who is found at his task when his master comes. . . . He will be put in charge of his master's property." When it finally dawns on us that we were born slaves, and are actually descended, not from royalty, but from the dust in the Maker's hand, we are properly oriented to appreciate God. We were property but He gives us our freedom to decide if He shall be our Father. This perspective makes us welcome work as a blessing, not a necessary evil to be resisted. If we can remember our place, we shall see we are but particles miraculously distinguished from the dust, favored with ears to hear the Voice of Purpose, with divinely delegated responsibility. Service offers us relief as a groaning tree giving up her fruit and makes us more precious to our Master. Working for Him is not work, it is freedom for appreciation and the prelude to a more dazzling "weight of glory." For, to our amazement, "It is in giving that we receive," it is "in dying that we are born." The cross is so much lighter than we thought; obedience suits us better than we could believe. The arrangement of His inheritance makes us ashamed we can do no better than our best in reply. To the outsider, "everything" must seem quite a price to pay for Christianity. But in the light of God's "everything," it is nothing at all—it is the least we can do and live with our conscience and not be suffocated with unexpressed gratitude.

THERE was a rich man, clad in purple and fine linen, who lived sumptuously every day. Outside his door lay a poor man called Lazarus; he was a mass of ulcers, and fain to feed on the crumbs that fell from the rich man's table. (The very dogs used to come and lick his ulcers.) Now it happened that the poor man died, and he was carried by the angels to Abraham's bosom. The rich man died too, and was buried. And as he was being tortured in Hades, he raised his eyes and saw Abraham far away with Lazarus in his bosom; so he called out, 'Father Abraham, take pity on me, send Lazarus to dip his finger-tip in water and cool my tongue, for I am in anguish in these flames.' But Abraham said, 'Remember, my son, you got all the bliss when you were alive, just as Lazarus got the ills of life; he is in comfort now, and you in anguish. Besides all that, a great gulf yawns between us and you, to keep back those who want to cross from us to you and also those who would pass from you to us.' Then he said, 'Well, father, I beg you to send him to my father's house, for I have five brothers; let him bear testimony to them, that they may not come to this place of torture as well.' 'They have got Moses and the prophets,' said Abraham, 'they can listen to them.' 'No, father Abraham,' he said, 'but if someone only goes to them from the dead, they will repent.' He said to him, 'If they will not listen to Moses and the prophets, they will not be convinced, not even if one rose from the dead.' "

LUKE 16:19-31, James Moffatt

19

The Rich Man and the Beggar

JESUS USUALLY PICKED up His parables firsthand from familiar objects He found around the house, at a wedding, or in a field. But this parable is an arresting exception. It takes us to the next world—a rare treat and very daring for so down-to-earth a Man to do. This time He took a dead-tired plot, as He taught Shakespeare to do, put some life into it, and put it to work for Him. "There was a certain rich man . . . and a certain beggar" —nothing new about that, but it was new when He got through, and it stayed that way. He took that burlesque theme and commanded it to tell nothing but the truth about life and death. Under His direction it was no one-night stand, but has played continuously to the stands of time ever since. He put something into this story most men do not see in life until the day they know they are going to die.

By its light we can see the next world standing by, waiting, watching, reacting to every move we make here. This illustration is not hypnotic entertainment, but a call to arms to meet the emergency of existence. The story has been known to make men lose sleep, to shock them to safety. It was this story that shook Albert Schweitzer into Africa, for he thought that's who his Lazarus was, and the story made him feel that sorry for the beggar—made him afraid he might be Dives, himself. Jesus did not take the perennial, painful contrast between wealth and poverty peacefully sitting down, but exposed it, remorselessly, for the sake of every sleeping Dives and starving Lazarus.

He arranged the story into a one-act play to fit a tiny stage for a cast of three: Dives, a rich man; Lazarus, a beggar; and Father Abraham, speaking for God in heaven. There are three scenes.

The first scene is a blow. Dives is dressed in royal purple. He is wearing the finest linen, and he is feasting sumptuously—it says he does this every day. Just outside the palatial gates of this man's splendid mansion lies a ghastly sight—Lazarus. The poor wretch has deteriorated to such a state that he has to be carried there each day. He is covered with sores and scabs, which the dogs are licking through the rags, and is so far gone he is actually glad to get Dives' garbage. The parable explains he specifically longs for the crust the rich man uses to wipe his mouth.

Like most of the shady characters in Jesus' drama, Dives does not bear the slightest resemblance to the vaudeville villain. He is not a Silas Marner type of miser but "richly fed and living merrily." He is not mean, for he hospitably lets the unsightly Lazarus lie around his house as long as he wants to, which is more than we can say of many men today. And Lazarus is living high enough on the table scraps to keep him coming back for more. Without doubt, Dives is a decent, law-abiding, leading citizen. Jesus makes Dives look respectable, like a good mixer, a hard worker, who goes to church, gives to charity, and is good to his neighbors. Jesus draws Dives too close to any audience for comfort.

The second scene jumps on ahead to heaven. Each man is dead. This is something that Jesus almost never does, and even here He definitely does not mean for any photograph to be taken. This is a parable, not as someone has said, "Baedeker's Guide to the next world." Jesus never cheated as some Peeping Toms have tried to do by pretending to give us a peek at something no man may see and live—we are not ready. The blinding glory of His heaven is none of our business yet. "Eye hath not seen, nor ear heard . . . the things which God hath prepared."

But while Jesus did not add to our knowledge of the next world, this makes us infinitely more aware of it and makes sure we know everything there is for us to know. Dives, despite a big funeral, lands in torment below. And Lazarus, after suffering the last indignity of being denied a decent burial, is lifted gently to heaven by ministering angels. The two men wake up over there clear-headed. They remember everything that has happened, recognize each other; death did not change the rules, but made the men change places. Dives is in terrible pain. Lazarus is out of his misery and safe at last in the bosom of Abraham. Heaven and hell are definitely divided up, but heaven is not a haven of uninterrupted rest. They can hear hell from there. In fact, Abraham can hear Dives crying. And Dives is not so far gone he can't defend himself. He is, for the first time in his life, working for pardon, praying for mercy, having to plead for just a little drop of water. Dives cries out with parched lips and burning tongue: "Father Abraham have mercy on me, and send Lazarus that he may dip the tip of his finger in water and cool my tongue; for I am in anguish in this flame."

What, we ask, is Dives, of all people, doing down in hell? This part of the picture is difficult for any rich man to appreciate. This appears at first to be the poor man's parable. But this is not indiscriminate damnation of the wealthy and a sweeping campaign promise of "sunlight and roses" for every son of want. We know Jesus well enough to know He did not suffer from class prejudice. His affection for a man is not inversely proportionate to his purse. Riches can be blessing instead of curse. Just look at Father Abraham, who on earth had everything a man could ask for. Poverty is not good, necessarily. Beggars can be born of bitterness and lazy bones.

There is nothing wrong with Dives, nothing, that is, except that Dives didn't care a finger snap for Lazarus. The damning evidence against Dives is that he could have a good time all the time that wretched bag of bones was out there groaning, dying, on his doorstep. It is this innocent-looking aloofness that propriety approves, this untouched neutrality and irresponsible disinterest for a man in trouble that Jesus dynamites as the earthworks of the devil. It is no sin to be rich. It is a sin to be rich and not have the heart for it. Dives' criminal act was overlooking Lazarus. He was hauled into hell for a clean-shaven heartlessness.

Lazarus, even after that last turn of the screw, never complained. He was "glad" to get the garbage. But the point of the parable is not his piety, but his pitifulness. Dives probably didn't know what a likeable chap Lazarus was, but he did know his need and that was the only clue he needed. Dives might not have had any miracle drugs, but in God's eyes Lazarus needed more than that. He needed Dives, he needed personal attention. Dives is "called on the carpet" because he came to earth and left without ever looking straight into Lazarus' eyes. He left his mess for someone else to clean up. God in heaven hurried to make up for lost time, and had to do Dives' job for him. Dives did not belong in a holy place where that kind of thing went on; he had no training, no practice for it. He had lost his life through no fault of his own, so much as by default.

And when Dives took his complaint to the Supreme Court, Abraham announced the verdict gently but firmly: "Son, remember that thou in thy lifetime received thy good things and Lazarus in like manner evil things"; "Son," he said, "you've had your heaven." We take our pick: This or that. Dives decided a bird in the hand was better and took today—in his own way. He could have used his means as a means of transportation—by taking better care of Lazarus and learning to live a better life. But he turned that heaven down to get a little peace and quiet here. Abraham tried to get his attention: "Son, remember. . . ." "Remember"—but Dives didn't even know enough to know what he had done, wasn't even grateful for earth in hell. Abraham would have to help him look for something missing in his past. Dives had not yet made Marley's momentous discovery. Marley was no example either on earth, but hell made an example of him—to Scrooge. For all the frightening ball and chains, he returned morally sensitive, saying things earth simply could not get him to say—or see. And when uneasy old Ebenezer risked the compliment: "You were always a good man of business, Jacob," the ghost screamed: "Business! Mankind was my business. The common welfare was my business; charity, mercy, forbearance, and benevolence, were, all, my business. The dealings of my trade were but a drop of water in the comprehensive ocean of my business."

Hell might be able to do as much for Dives.

Abraham had to say something else to Dives. It was hard to

say—and hear. "Besides all this, between us and you there is a great gulf fixed." Who did it? Where did hell come from? God didn't do it in the Apostles' Creed. Dives dug his share, day after day, inch by erosive inch, drip by drip, until by his accumulated indifference and divergent interest, he had alienated himself from God by a Grand Canyon's worth. Dives had been learning, practicing all his life, how to live on "the wrong side of the sky." The selfish business Dives had developed on earth, legitimate though it was in mortal eyes, had no future. He gambled on what he thought was a sure bet—and lost. Death to Lazarus meant salvation. To Dives it was the end; in the twinkling of an eye, everything he had worked for, was interested in, was wiped out. His securities were not safe from the moth, they were subject to corrosion, were something "thieves could break in and steal." Heaven to him was completely foreign territory.

"Besides all this, between us and you there is a great gulf fixed," and now Abraham brought home to Dives the worst to come: "that none may cross over." Dives had had his chance and it was gone—forever. No Scrooge has been able to scare away this requirement with a "Humbug." That last breath rattles with the finality with which this story is filled. Death marks the end, not of an installment, but a book, when a man must stand his white-glove inspection. Dante had these words on the mouth of his hell: "Abandon all hope ye who enter here." That is terribly hard to take for men born and bred on Christian mercy. But we have all seen enough hell here to know it's there. We know enough of life to know no man can get away with murder. Somewhere, sometime, justice will be done, and it will not be a laugh. Earth is wasted effort if it's just for fun, just fooling, and not official, final. The devout have never taken this lightly—it is only the undisciplined who want off lightly. Good men have thanked God for being good enough to be definite about that day. We can never pout there as Dives did, that we were never told in time "that none may cross over." America, America! any three-square-meals-a-day American ditchdigger, every student of divinity may be Dives not yet dead, but carrying around instead the dreadful blessed secret of this story safely in his head.

Is Dives done for? David cried: "If I make my bed in hell, behold, thou art there." He also said: "Thou wilt not leave my soul in hell." And Christ's love, if not all His lines, nourish a hope, human if illegitimate, that threatens to put the Inferno out eventually. Christ descended into hell Himself. Could the place ever be the same again? "That none may cross over," yet He crossed over. The Creed claims that He went there first after He left here. Did He make a path for Dives' descendants to follow? "I am he that liveth . . . and have the keys of hell and of death." It is so hard for loving hearts to believe that heaven could ever resist a Dives coming with a Lazarus on his arm. But would Dives do any differently if he had it all to do over again? We do not know. But much modern defiance of hell dies down upon devout reflection. Hell has to be irreversible somehow to be hell. And without the dreadful decisiveness it brings to death, this life loses its epic cruciality.

But now Dives was only digging himself in deeper. As we might expect, he had a last request to make: "Then I beg you, father, to send him [Lazarus] to my father's house [he hadn't grasped Lazarus' sudden elevation nor the fact that hell is not the place to ask for special favors], for I have five brothers, so that he may warn them lest they also come into this place of torment." He was hunting desperately for Abraham's soft spot, as if to say no one had ever told this poor little fellow about what was coming to him. It was his last stand.

Abraham's answer gives us God's view on this and it is as convincing as it is startling. "But Abraham said; they have Moses and the prophets; let them hear them." Dives, still arguing, says his dying words: "Nay Father Abraham, but if one go to them from the dead, they will repent." But Abraham has the last word. "If they do not hear Moses and the prophets, neither will they be convinced if someone should rise from the dead." It is a strange story for One to tell who would one day rise Himself. But if a man pays no attention to the prophets, then a resurrection would be wasted on him. Men are not converted by their senses nor clever logic. If Jesus Christ were to visit us today, it is doubtful if any doubter would be very disturbed by the experience. It would cause talk, arouse curiosity, create far more controversy than conversions. Men who are ready to believe can find enough in the Bible and in their hearts already to believe. And if they are immune to that "still small voice" not a million miracles could convince them. The human heart is so resourcefully stubborn, Calvin said in desperation, totally depraved. It can ingeniously sabotage the sturdiest faith or rationalize away any idea standing in the way of what it wants to believe. A man believes what he wants to believe, and until he wants to believe in God, God Himself must wait.

How long will He wait? The Bible does its best to make us hurry up. It sets a deadline and some standards to get out of us everything that is in us, as soon as possible. It tells us in the nicest way that judgment is none of our business. All its sternness is kindness, its way of saying we have nothing else to worry about except right now, so we can keep our minds on our work, throw everything we have into the fight we have on our hands this minute, and leave the rest to heaven.

'How can I describe the people of this generation? What are they like? They are like children sitting in the market-place and shouting at each other,

"We piped for you and you would not dance."

"We wept and wailed, and you would not mourn."

For John the Baptist came neither eating bread nor drinking wine, and you say, "He is possessed." The Son of Man came eating and drinking, and you say, "Look at him! a glutton and a drinker, a friend of tax-gatherers and sinners!" And yet God's wisdom is proved right by all who are her children.'

LUKE 7:31-35 (also MATTHEW 11:16-19), New English Bible

✠

THEREFORE whosoever heareth these sayings of mine, and doeth them, I will liken him unto a wise man, which built his house upon a rock: And the rain descended, and the floods came, and the winds blew, and beat upon that house; and it fell not: for it was founded upon a rock. And every one that heareth these sayings of mine, and doeth them not, shall be likened unto a foolish man, which built his house upon the sand: And the rain descended, and the floods came, and the winds blew, and beat upon that house; and it fell: and great was the fall of it.

MATTHEW 7:24-27 (also LUKE 6:46-49), King James Version

✠

WHEN the Son of man shall come in his glory, and all the holy angels with him, then shall he sit upon the throne of his glory: And before him shall be gathered all nations; and he shall separate them one from another, as a shepherd divideth his

157

sheep from the goats: And he shall set the sheep on his right hand, but the goats on the left. Then shall the King say unto them on his right hand, Come, ye blessed of my Father, inherit the kingdom prepared for you from the foundation of the world: For I was an hungred, and ye gave me meat: I was thirsty, and ye gave me drink: I was a stranger, and ye took me in: Naked, and ye clothed me: I was sick, and ye visited me: I was in prison, and ye came unto me. Then shall the righteous answer him, saying, Lord, when saw we thee an hungred, and fed thee? or thirsty, and gave thee drink? When saw we thee a stranger, and took thee in? or naked, and clothed thee? Or when saw we thee sick, or in prison, and came unto thee? And the King shall answer and say unto them, Verily I say unto you, Inasmuch as ye have done it unto one of the least of these my brethren, ye have done it unto me. Then shall he say also unto them on the left hand, Depart from me, ye cursed, into everlasting fire, prepared for the devil and his angels: For I was an hungred, and ye gave me no meat: I was thirsty, and ye gave me no drink: I was a stranger, and ye took me not in: naked, and ye clothed me not: sick, and in prison, and ye visited me not. Then shall they also answer him, saying, Lord, when saw we thee an hungred, or athirst, or a stranger, or naked, or sick, or in prison, and did not minister unto thee? Then shall he answer them, saying, Verily I say unto you, Inasmuch as ye did it not to one of the least of these, ye did it not to me. And these shall go away into everlasting punishment: but the righteous into life eternal.

MATTHEW 25:31-46, King James Version

20

The Petulant Children
The Wise and Foolish Builders
The Last Judgment

WHAT DOES JESUS really think of us? In a moment mixed with good humor and grim despair He exclaimed: "How can I describe . . . this generation?" Then this parable gave Him away. These people are like petulant children who won't play any game suggested. They won't play weddings and they won't play funerals. " 'We piped for you and you would not dance.' 'We wept and wailed, and you would not mourn.' For John the Baptist came neither eating bread nor drinking wine, and you say, 'He is possessed.' The Son of Man came eating and drinking and you say, 'Look at him a glutton and a drinker.' "

Mankind, Jesus decided, did not want God in any shape or form. For God sent John, strict, ascetic, funereal, but men said he must be mad. Then God sent His Son who loved life, good friends, food and drink, His life like a wedding party, and men despised Him as a glutton and a drunkard. Men seem determined to give genuine religion a bad name—to make fun of it, make it look ridiculous, impossible, blasphemous, in order to have a good excuse. If it is stern they say, "fire and brimstone," if it is kind they say, "effeminate," if it is alive they shout derisively, "Salvation Army." The church is supposed to be full of hypocrites, and if they take back a sinner it is said that they stand for nothing. Ministers are too young, too old, too conservative, too liberal, just plain gullible or crafty Elmer Gantrys. If the church is quiet it is nothing but a monastery, but if it speaks out it is meddling with politics. Faith is old-maidish or too modern, superstition or heresy. The service is too high, too low, too long, too short—all of which criticism, according to Jesus, is a subversive campaign to smear and escape God; not even John nor Jesus could make God presentable to such a society.

Jesus was also indicting adults for not growing up, for playing church—"They are like children." Religion for so many men is not something that uses them, but something they use, to get ahead, get cheered up, get a little relief from guilt and a little spiritual shot in the arm. The creeds and vestments are taken out then put back in the box. Worship is a few minutes of peace instead of an hour of decision that leads to peace. Theologians toy with ideas, and preachers play with fire. A father feels that a little religion would be good for his child, which is flirting with the command "with all thy heart." Men do not think of themselves as disciples who are to endure to the end; they prefer a less demanding phrase like "members in good standing." This cut-rate faith is not a forward march following the Master but a routine of confession, fasting, communion. Church is a game, a bingo of charities, rummage; it means nice little things to do, but nothing drastic, everything is under control—like state-supervised gambling—so no one can lose very much. Isaiah reeled from the temple after facing God crying, "Woe is me! for I am undone . . . for mine eyes have seen the King." Protestants have reduced this to pledge cards and mimeographing. Church attendance has become an elective and comes under weekly discussion now. Christianity is not "more love to thee, O Christ" day after day, deed by deed, every step of the way; it is an audited course offered by an institution. Ministers soft-pedal it, setting up straw men, shadow boxing, getting the acting letter-perfect, just as children do in playing games—but it is not real. It is a diversion from God.

If that parable of the petulant children tells what Jesus thinks of us, the second parable about the two builders tells what He thinks about life. Men may be fooling; life is not. He chose this parable to close His Sermon on the Mount, for it shows how desperate life becomes and how desperately our future hangs on following His instructions. "And every one that heareth these sayings of mine, and doeth them not, shall be likened unto a foolish man, which built his house upon the sand: and the rain descended, and the floods came, and the winds blew, and beat upon that house; and it fell: and great was the fall of it."

Jesus loved us too much to be anything but brutally honest. He thought we ought to know there was a storm brewing, and He thought we would want to know now while we were working on the foundation that to build upon sand is a grave mistake. So He forced us to think about the future, not so we'll forget the present, but so we won't forget what it's meant for. Our day, of course, doesn't like authority. It likes to say, "It seems to me"—which is a good thing for men to say. But the Bible never speaks that way. It acts as if it knows. "He taught them as one having authority." No man was ever more humble, no one ever got lower down—on His knees to the last, washing and drying the feet of His men. But He was so absolutely sure that what He said was true, that for our sakes He announced that those who heard Him and did nothing about it were fools making castles in the sand with their very lives. Few men have ever questioned His judgment. No one has even tried to disprove Him. Most men have just gone on playing in the sand.

The parable likens our life to a house. What are we building it out of? The way we spend our time. Some consume time in hatred, lust, jealousy, envy—acids which would eat up rock. Who of us would care to have our hours of unworthy daydreaming tabulated—time spent, wasted, burned, wrecked, thinking thoughts, relishing desires we should not have had, taking up precious time we could have used laying up stone.

But think, not of the acid eating at our life like cancer but of the shifting sand we're using. Christ was not as exercised about our evil as about our filler (the long TV evenings of nothingness that are going into us). The lives Jesus saw everywhere about Him were not taken up with sin so much as nonsense. The victim in this parable is not a villain, but a crazy fool, building his life on trash. Most men are not aggressive criminals, but nit-wits throwing their lives away on candy, cars, record sales, attendance, wasting their time on themselves. Here's a man that's just asking for it, with no more sense than to put his wife, his son, or his job on a pedestal. Ty Cobb, a legend in American base-ball, indicted himself before he died. He confessed: "You cannot eat baseball and sleep baseball and study baseball year after year and just stop like that." That's what Jesus is trying to say in this story. You can't put everything into anything (except what God has said to) and expect to weather the time when your baseball days or professional days are over. If the only thing we have read religiously all our lives is the newspaper, if we know the statistics on each All-American better than we know what Jesus said and did, and can tell what the President's wife wore to the Inaugural Ball but can't think of a beatitude, God help our folly.

There is nothing wrong with sports or fashions; Jesus came that we might have life and have it more abundantly and He would have gone to our games and kept in style. But what is foolish is trying to fit God into a corner of our ball park or office. That is the scandal Christ exposed. The job and the game and the house and the wife were made to fit into God's plan, and men have gotten it backwards, building upside down—paying the mortgage first, the bills first, what they want first, putting off the foundation until they can get some time. This parable does not question our sin so much as our sanity and our inexcusable workmanship. Men are simply not putting their lives up to stay. This frantic rush to live higher than we should, beyond our means, to cultivate the right friends, read what others are reading, just doesn't have what it takes. The first puff of pain, the first unexpected shift in plans and that house will go down like a stack of cards. The ultimate question life asks of each of us is not if we can play bridge, baseball, or the stock market, but how well we built our life. And if a man builds on sand, no matter how many ivy-covered degrees he holds, how far he goes, if God is not under him, he'll just have that much farther to fall; the next little squall could take away his fragile treasures till he has nothing left to live for, and he cracks up in broken pride or suicide.

"Therefore whosoever heareth these sayings of mine, and doeth them, I will liken him unto a wise man, which built his house upon a rock." Jesus sacrificed His life to give us rock. There is only one sure thing to build on for any man and that is Him. Everything going on about us may have to do with scaffolding, with keeping house, the pressing choice of colors, the distracting hustle and bustle going on above ground. All that will give us plenty of excuses, but it won't build foundation. The wise man has to have that first. Everything he does will be subordinate to that. He will see that everything he buys, reads, thinks about, will be a means of strengthening his tie to God. He will treat the Bible as his handbook, not an heirloom. He will practice prayer until he's expert in it. The church will not be a nagging duty to him, but a structural force, a comforting joy. He will become informed, acquire a taste for faith, until he is at home in that atmosphere, accustomed to looking at life in that light. And this basic orientation will give him a sense of security. He will gain confidence, not in something that can be pulled from under him at any moment, but in a sure thing. He will not go overboard for things that should be taken in stride and he will be able to enjoy all the good things he has, not with suppressed guilt feelings, but as blessings. Each day he will feel his way with faith; he won't try to fasten a little religion on the back of his life, late in life, to salve his conscience and make believe he's made up for it.

"Now, everyone who listens to these words of mine and acts upon them will be like a sensible man." The gospel is not merely an announcement, it is an order—"remember me," "come to me," "pray," "comfort," "help," "love," "forgive." Christianity begins with a noun, but it comes (and it never comes to anything till it does) to the verb "do." We may not be able to understand all of the Bible, but Mark Twain confessed for the sturdiest skeptic when he declared that what bothered him most about the Bible is what he could understand. "Who will go for us?"

"And the floods came, and the wind blew." Faith will not stop the storm from coming, but it can take it. If through the years we have eaten, studied, practiced the essential things, if we have drawn on the wealth of example, made a well-beaten path to the door of the Almighty in the daytime, stored up reserves of moral energy, built broad and deep and solid, we shall not be so quick to press the panic button, not so suspicious; we will not be so important to ourselves, not too anxious, not so easily shattered. What would happen to a man if the company or the wife said, "I'm through with you," if his reputation were ruined, his savings gone up in smoke, his health broken or his dearest kidnaped, and he was left deserted, dying? According to Christ, everything depends on whether he built his life on rock. If he did, the storm will test him and in the darkness he may lose his temper, his patience, even his faith, but not for long, for he shall be safe and know that all shall be safe in the eye of the storm. "Who trusts in God's unchanging love builds on the rock that naught can move."

The last parable is called the Parable of the Last Judgment. It is the last one He ever told, and while He was telling it He was sitting on the Mount of Olives and staring into the jaws of death just a few hours off. What will we be thinking of on our dying day? It reminded Him of this story. Hemingway couldn't see anything beyond; Christ saw a breathtaking sight, and important business coming up, "When the Son of man shall come in his glory." Rome was about to step on Him but it did not interrupt His plane of thought. Was it madness? He went on, "And all the holy angels with him, then shall he sit upon the throne of his glory." This manger-born and dying criminal carpenter speaking quietly, but so convincingly of His throne, that this late word has reached the rest of us. "And before him," Jesus continued, "shall be gathered all nations." And then the Master came to this astounding assertion: "And he shall separate them one from another, as a shepherd divideth his sheep from the goats."

"For we shall all stand before the judgment seat of Christ." How could He—they—say such a thing, unless it is the truth? "If it were not so I would have told you." If we cannot believe Him, then, whom can we believe? He seems higher than His higher critics. "Lord, I believe; help thou mine unbelief."

But are men to be divided so neatly? Palestinian sheep were white and goats were black, easily identified. Is that true of men? But Christ can read the heart quite clearly. No one is perfect, but some are trying, hoping, wishing, praying, and working to be perfect, just as plainly as the rest have decided not to.

Then Jesus explains God's measuring stick. The whole question of our destination depends on whether or not we were kind to Him on earth, but this means more than kind words praying. It means that "Anything you did not do for one of the least of these my brothers, you did it not unto me."

Both heaven and hell will be a surprise. The righteous did not know they were being kind. They were kind unconsciously. The goats don't know how oblivious they have been to suffering and starvation. Kindness comes naturally to the saints, so modestly, so quickly, they cannot remember when they did it. The Pharisees think they are so much better, they presume they have been superior in kindness as in their own mind, but they are blind on that side and have missed the men who needed them. Their heaven may be a surprise to them and turn out to be hell.

This kindness is not a check written to charity. It is a way of life, where a man is looking for trouble to remedy as much as looking out for himself. He spends some time searching for his man to help as well as carrying on his trade—which is a help. This man has a light burning in the window, and has gone out often with the lantern, out of kindness. This kindness is not flattery, nor a handout, but intelligent. It is kind enough to be ingenious, imaginative; it is not obnoxiously noticeable, but quiet.

But if hell comes as a surprise to some of us standing smugly in a pulpit or a pew, we cannot complain as Dives did that we were never told. The final examination will not be sprung on us. We already know in advance the very questions that will be asked. He gave them to us in this story just before He left. Our Man has given us the answers, and given us so fair a warning, such generous offers of His continuing help, that anything more would waste God's time.

We cannot say no one knows what happens after death. Some things are painfully clear. They are going to ask for our prison record. No, not the time we did forcibly, but the time we freely spent for our brothers, His brothers, His sake. How many hungry mouths have we fed how many times? Whose fault is it if we don't even know any? The trouble is not in our set. How many suffering, naked people have we clothed with dignity and happiness as well as shoes? Will heaven be mobbed with men eager to sing our praises tomorrow and testify to all the sacrifices we made for them today? How are we doing with strangers? Is our home a haven for them or is the stranger excluded? Feared? Have we taken more precautions, spent more in locks, fences, insurance, to protect ourselves against the stranger than we have taken measures to make him welcome? Will our friendship here to the stranger be judged above as an exception to the rule of our life, or a habit we got into with a passion? How much of our life has been taken up with visiting the sick?—not our sick friends, but "the least of these, my brethren?" This is our business if we mean business with our life. Is your life unfinished business? Or not yet begun?

Through these three parables, through all the parables He ever told, throbs the note of urgency at white-hot heat. He gave us what He knew every way He could think of to say it in these lovely little stories—to alert us to the terrible immediacy, and importance, of the next few moments. This is all life has for anyone—to alarm us to action before it is too late. Just think of the time, the love, the blood and tears and "all the light of sacred story" He put into these precious lights "to save us all from Satan's power when we were gone astray." You and I occupy special seats today, for some men long ago heard only one parable and that was all they needed. But time has carefully kept and polished them just for us, so we could hear them all again and again.

> He has sounded forth the trumpet that shall never call retreat;
> He is sifting out the hearts of men before His Judgment seat;
> Oh, be swift my soul, to answer Him! be jubilant, my feet!

Bibliography

The Interpreter's Bible, Vols. VII and VIII. Nashville: Abingdon-Cokesbury Press, 1952.

A. B. Bruce, *The Parabolic Teaching of Christ*. London: Hodder & Stoughton, Ltd., MDCCCXCV.

George A. Buttrick, *The Parables of Jesus*. New York: Harper & Brothers, 1928.

A. T. Cadoux, *Parables of Jesus*. New York: The Macmillan Co., 1931.

C. H. Dodd, *Parables of the Kingdom*. New York: Charles Scribner's Sons, 1960.

Marcus Dods, *The Parables of Our Lord*. London: Hodder & Stoughton, Ltd., MDCCCLXXXVI.

William M. Taylor, *The Parables of Our Saviour*. London: Hodder & Stoughton, Ltd., MDCCCLXXXIX.

Richard Chenevix Trench, *Notes on the Parables of Our Lord*. New Jersey: Fleming H. Revell Company.

Sources

Page	Line	
11	16	Proverbs 9:10, KJV.
11	31	Luke 15:7, RSV.
12	8	Luke 15:11, KJV.
12	21	Luke 15:12, KJV.
12	28	*Ibid.*
13	11	Luke 15:13, KJV.
13	17	*Ibid.*
13	24	Luke 15:14, KJV.
13	32	Luke 15:15, KJV.
13	35	Luke 15:16, KJV.
14	18	Luke 15:18, KJV.
14	19	Luke 15:17, KJV.
14	27	Luke 15:21, KJV.
15	1	Luke 15:20, KJV.
16	9	Matthew 21:31, NEB.
16	27	Luke 15:29, 30, NEB.
17	12	Luke 15:31,32, NEB.
22	11	Matthew 21:37,38, ASV.
23	11	William Cullen Bryant, "Thanatopsis."
23	20	Matthew 21:41, ASV.
23	31	John 9:4, KJV.
24	11	Luke 12:47,48, RSV.
24	28	Amos 3:2, ASV.
24	32	Matthew 11:21,22, RSV.
25	4	Luke 12:48, RSV.
25	10	Paraphrased from Fedor Dostoevski's *Brothers Karamazov.*
26	9	Mark 13:35, KJV.
26	19	Matthew 18:14, KJV.
29	2	Matthew 19:24, RSV.
29	9	Matthew 19:26, RSV.
29	19	Matthew 19:27, RSV.
29	25	Matthew 19:30, RSV.
30	1	Matthew 20:1, RSV.
30	26	Matthew 20:10, RSV.
30	29	Matthew 20:11,12, RSV.
31	1	Matthew 20:13-15, RSV.
31	10	Isaiah 55:8, KJV.
32	25	Ephesians 2:9, KJV.
33	28	Thomas Gray, "Elegy Written in a Country Churchyard."
33	31	Luke 21:1, RSV.

SOURCES

Page	Line	
37	2	Luke 11:1, KJV.
37	7	Luke 18:1, RSV.
37	14	Luke 11:7, NEB.
37	22	Luke 11:11, NEB.
38	18	From the hymn, "Strong Son of God, Immortal Love," by Alfred Tennyson.
38	21	Psalm 121:4, KJV.
38	22	Luke 18:19, RSV.
39	9	Luke 18:5, NEB.
39	36	Genesis 32:26, KJV.
40	7	Luke 22:44, KJV.
40	26	Isaiah 40:31, KJV.
41	5	From *The Stargazer*, Zsolt de Horsany, trans. by Paul Tabor, G. P. Putnam's Sons, 1939, p. 256.
46	36	Luke 7:39, RSV.
47	9	Luke 7:40, RSV.
47	10	*Ibid.*
47	17	Luke 7:41, RSV.
47	24	Luke 7:43, RSV.
47	31	Matthew 4:7, KJV.
48	11	Romans 3:23, KJV.
48	24	Luke 7:44-47, ASV.
48	34	Matthew 18:21,22, ASV.
49	9	George Buttrick, *The Parables of Jesus*, p. 100.
49	14	Matthew 18:25-27, ASV.
49	26	Luke 15:19, RSV.
50	6	Matthew 18:29-31, NEB.
50	12	Matthew 18:33, ASV.
50	17	Matthew 18:35, RSV.
50	28	Paraphrase of a story from an article by John Rord Lagemann in *The Reader's Digest*, March 1961, p. 41.
51	19	Matthew 6:14, KJV.
51	21	William Shakespeare, *The Merchant of Venice*, Act IV, Sc. 1.
55	1	John 18:36, KJV.
55	24	Mark 4:28, NEB.
57	7	Matthew 16:18, KJV.
57	33	I Kings 19:12, KJV.
58	5	Psalm 46:10, KJV.
58	9	Sir John Seeley, *Ecce Homo* (E. P. Dutton & Co., 1908), p. 264.
58	19	Zechariah 4:6, KJV.

Page	Line	
58	28	John 1:5, RSV.
58	31	Matthew 18:14, RSV.
59	4	Matthew 13:33, RSV.
61	10	Matthew 13:44, NEB.
61	24	I Corinthians 12:31, RSV.
63	30	II Corinthians 4:17, KJV.
63	32	Hebrews 12:2, KJV.
64	15	Genesis 2:17, KJV.
67	5	Matthew 5:33,34, KJV.
67	15	Luke 18:12, KJV.
67	17	Acts 17:6, RSV.
68	14	Luke 5:34, RSV.
68	18	Matthew 9:16, RSV.
68	29	Luke 5:37, RSV.
70	13	Matthew 5:17, ASV.
70	14	Luke 5:39, ASV.
70	16	Matthew 13:52, ASV.
70	25	Hebrews 13:8, KJV.
71	4	I Corinthians 2:9, KJV.
71	26	Revelation 21:1, KJV.
73	1	Matthew 13:24,25, ASV.
73	25	Matthew 13:27, NEB.
74	6	I John 1:5, KJV.
74	8	James 1:17, ASV.
74	21	Matthew 13:29, RSV.
74	35	Luke 13:23,24, KJV.
75	13	Matthew 13:30, RSV.
75	16	Psalm 1:4, KJV.
76	6	Romans 12:19, RSV.
76	8	Matthew 13:30, RSV.
76	8	Matthew 13:29, RSV.
76	12	Matthew 13:30, RSV.
76	26	Matthew 6:13, KJV.
77	17	James Russell Lowell, "The Present Crisis."
82	5	Matthew 22:2,3, RSV.
84	33	Matthew 22:7-10, NEB.
86	13	Luke 13:3, KJV.
86	15	Clifford Bax.
90	1	Luke 5:5, KJV.
90	2	Matthew 13:58, KJV.
90	14	Luke 16:31, KJV.
90	16	Mark 4:24, KJV.

SOURCES

Page	Line	
164	2	Isaiah 6:8, KJV.
164	19	From the hymn "If Thou But Suffer God To Guide Thee," by Georg Neumark.
165	3	Romans 14:10, KJV.
165	5	John 14:2, KJV.
165	7	Mark 9:24, KJV.
166	35	From the hymn "In the Cross of Christ I Glory," by John Bowring.
166	36	From the traditional English carol, "God Rest You Merry."
167	6	From "The Battle Hymn of the Republic," by Julia Ward Howe.